What Really in *Ha...*

Madness in Elsinore is Sanity in Southwark

F.H.G.Percy has produced an indispensable addition to annotated texts of *Hamlet*, all of which reveal uncertainty or ignorance of the meaning of many textual enigmas. His examination of Hamlet's 'mad' remarks – he never talks nonsense – made in seriousness or jest, determines a continuous thread of topical allusions, readily understood by the audience at the theatre, prompted by Polonius's signal to them in his asides: 'Though this be madness, yet there is method in 't', and 'How pregnant sometimes his replies are! A happiness that madness hits on, which reason and sanity could not so prosperously be delivered of.'.

Here such cruxes as 'You're a fishmonger', 'I am but mad north-north-west', 'I know a hawk from a handsaw', 'the hobby-horse is forgot' and many more editorial problems have been solved.

No reader, playgoer, student, teacher, actor, even director of *Hamlet* can fail to improve their understanding of the play by reading this fresh, original yet scholarly examination of the most daunting drama of the English stage.

Also by F.H.G.Percy
WHITGIFT SCHOOL A History

THE
Tragicall Historie of
HAMLET,

Prince of Denmarke.

By William Shakespeare.

Newly imprinted and enlarged to almost as much againe as it was, according to the true and perfect Coppie.

AT LONDON,
Printed by I. R. for N. L. and are to be sold at his shoppe vnder Saint Dunstons Church in

Title page of *Hamlet*, Q2

What Really Happened in *Hamlet*

Madness in Elsinore is Sanity in Southwark

F. H. G. Percy

Rosmic Books

Copyright © F.H.G.Percy 2006

*The right of F.H.G.Percy to be identified
as the author of this book has been
asserted by him in accordance with
the Copyright, Designs and Patents Act 1988*

First published in Great Britain 2006
ISBN 0-9513583-2-4

Published by Rosmic Books
Bookends, Lewes Road, Horsted Keynes,
West Sussex RH17 7DP

Printed by JEM Digital Printing
Staplehurst Road,
Sittingbourne, Kent ME10 2NH

CONTENTS

Introduction	11
Textual Commentary	15
Horatio's Status	61
Addendum: Wit and Gifts	65
Conclusion	73

Appendices

I	Imagery Associated with Livery Companies	77
II	Livery	88
III	Heraldry	89
IV	Weaponry	91
V	Social Status	93
VI	Other Imagery	97
VII	Some Nicknames used by Queen Elizabeth I	98

Select Bibliography	100

Indexes

Persons	103
Place Names	106
Annotations	108
Acknowledgements	111

ILLUSTRATIONS

Title page of *Hamlet*, Q2	Frontispiece
Sir John Leman (*The Royal Collection © 2006 Her Majesty Queen Elizabeth II*)	16
Sir Francis Bacon (*National Portrait Gallery, London*)	25
Hatfield Old Palace (*by kind permission of The Marquess of Salisbury*)	26
King James I (*National Portrait Gallery, London*)	27
Sir Julius Caesar (*National Portrait Gallery, London*)	32
Sir Edward Hoby (*National Portrait Gallery, London*)	34
The Hoby Memorial, Bisham (*by kind permission of All Saints Church, Bisham*)	35
Sir Robert Cecil, Earl of Salisbury (*by kind permission of the Marquess of Salisbury*)	38
Robin Goodfellow (*British Library*)	41
Edward, Lord Zouche (*by kind permission of the Executors of Mrs P.A. Tritton, Parham House*)	47
Sir Edward Coke (*National Portrait Gallery, London*)	49
Sir William Dethick (*The College of Arms, London*)	51
Peter Bales's Enconium (*Lambeth Palace Archives*)	55
Henry, Prince of Wales (*National Portrait Gallery, London*)	56
Archbishop John Whitgift (*Whitgift Foundation*)	64
Title page of George Paule's *Life of Whitgift*	66
River Thames: Lambeth to Southwark (*Guildhall Library*)	68
Martin Jarvis and Roger, Lord Freeman in *Hamlet* (*Whitgift School Archives*)	76
Shakespeare's Coat of Arms (*New Temple Shalespeare 1922*)	90

To Mollie

who for more than sixty-five years of marriage

has given me her love, companionship,

support and encouragement

in all my endeavours

INTRODUCTION

For many people Shakespeare is the greatest Englishman that ever lived, of world-wide literary fame, whose works are not only a source of great delight but also a subject of scholarly interpretation, exposition and commentary, absorbing the attention of literary critics and amateur enthusiasts to a degree surpassing that given to any other author.

Yet Shakespeare remains an indistinct figure, with no contemporary biographer, no memoirist and only a few friends, such as Ben Jonson, to praise him ("I do honour his memory this side of idolatry"). Our knowledge of his physical appearance is limited to his posthumous bust in Stratford Church, the engraving in the First Folio, and the 'Chandos' portrait. Of his personal domestic and social life next to nothing is known, although many hands have tried to piece together a character for him from the depth of his own portrayals of human nature. No controversial remark or casual observation of any kind has been preserved. Professor Dover Wilson remarked: "As a dramatic poet, Shakespeare has no personality". As for his religious beliefs, Professor Patrick Collinson declared: "We cannot say".

Attempts have been made to discover in his works hidden references to topical events and people of his time, perhaps through some coded message that, once deciphered, will open up a secondary meaning or give an allegorical or symbolic reflection of the contemporary scene. For instance, Dr A L Rowse claimed to have identified The Dark Lady of the Sonnets; and 'Mr WH', the dedicatee, as the Earl of Southampton, whereas Dover Wilson settled for the Earl of Pembroke, and Professor Leslie Hotson proposed William Hatcliffe; for none of these is there any certainty.

Such clue-seeking is part of the great game of literary research and detection. Any attempt to penetrate and define the working of Shakespeare's mind and dramatic invention must be hazardous. He always has been and always will be enigmatic. "Others abide our question. Thou art free/.../Out-topping knowledge" remains as true now as ever it has done, despite many recent attempts to pluck out the heart of his mystery.

Elizabethan drama was little different from Greek or modern drama as a vehicle for satirical comment on people and events of the non-stage world, and many ambiguities, implications, similarities and allusions have been taken up by editors: the characters of Prospero, Falstaff, Malvolio and Polonius, for instance, the last being possibly a caricature of time-serving, scheming, spy-catching William Cecil, Lord Burghley, Elizabeth's First Secretary of State, who died in 1598. But a playwright would be daring indeed if he were to satirise openly any powerful living figure of the establishment, and Burghley's memory would be sacrosanct so long as his son Robert remained in power as his successor to the post of First Secretary to the monarch.

Shakespeare delighted in allusive word-play, which he expected to be comprehensible to a few of his audience and challenging to some others, although perhaps baffling to those who were content with 'dumbshow and noise'. Whatever the effect upon the playgoers, he took private pleasure in covert satire and in its evasion of the censors' attention.

Because there were no contemporary reviewers or dramatic critics, most of these arcane references remain obscure and even undetected. Some interpretations have been convincing; conjecture, sometimes unsubstantiated, can be conflicting and erroneous. The modern world, with its interest in celebrities prominent in the media, is in contrast with that of Shakespeare's time, in which the subjects of common gossip and scandal are unknown, for next to nothing was recorded.

Many of Shakespeare's plays are set in foreign parts: *A Midsummer's Night Dream* in Athens, *Twelfth Night* in Illyria and *Hamlet* in Denmark, but all are effectively set in England, a point many scholars are agreed upon. The names of several of the characters in *Hamlet* were changed between the First and Second Quartos, and now range among the classical, the Italian, the Teutonic and the fanciful, as if Denmark were an invented territory – a northern Europe *Erewhon*. Bearing in mind the strong indication that *Hamlet* may have been regarded on one level as an allegory of early Stuart England, coupled with the possibility that celebrities of the London scene may have been objects of satire, I looked for further indications in support of this conjecture.

In the Preface to his New Arden (1982) edition of Hamlet Professor Harold Jenkins expressed his problem of interpretation: "I have found the bigger task with *Hamlet* to be that of annotation. Like Dover Wilson before me, I have been surprised at how many passages in Shakespeare lack satisfactory exegesis. Some explanations handed on from editor to editor I believe to be quite wrong."

The textual references by act, scene and line, thus: I. i. 82, apply to the conflated editions of Q1, Q2 and Folio (F) in The New Penguin Shakespeare *Hamlet*, edited by T J B Spencer, 1980, reissued in the Penguin Shakespeare series in 2005. For footnotes I have also referred to The Arden Shakespeare *Hamlet*, edited by Harold Jenkins, 1982, and The Oxford Shakespeare *Hamlet*, edited by G R Hibberd, 1998. I have also used *The First Quarto of Hamlet*, edited by Kathleen O. Irace, in the New Cambridge Shakespeare series, 1998.

TEXTUAL COMMENTARY

I. i. 82
HORATIO: .... by **Fortinbras** of Norway,

The notion that **Fortinbras**, the man from the North, reflects the position of James I, also virtually an elected monarch, and the husband of a Danish princess into the bargain, has been frequently advanced by editors. It would not have been rejected by the audience, who were given the revised version of *Hamlet* of 1604, in which no disloyalty was discoverable; on the contrary, James was welcomed by a realm persuaded in his favour and relieved that Queen Elizabeth was dead.

But the Frenchified '**Fortinbras**' (**Fortenbrasse** in Q1) points unerringly to Archie **Armstrong**, James's Scottish court jester, favourite and *alter ego*, who accompanied the King to London where, like the Fool in *King Lear* (1608), he was on terms of tolerated, insolent familiarity with his royal master.

II. ii. 173

POLONIUS: Do you know me, my lord?
HAMLET: Excellent well. You are a **fishmonger**.
POLONIUS: Not I, my lord.
HAMLET: Then I would you were so honest a man.
POLONIUS: Honest, my lord?
HAMLET: Ay, sir. To be honest, as this world goes, is to be one man picked out of ten thousand.

To call a man a 'fishmonger' is on the face of it an insult, for fishmongers deal in smelly produce that soon begins to stink in decay.

The term was also slang for a lecher or a bawd. It is no wonder that

Polonius is startled. The exchange between the two men seems to involve more than a mere gibe at Polonius's expense, whether delivered in 'madness' or not, for why should 'honesty' be immediately introduced to revoke implied corruption, unless in heavy irony?

Having for long accepted the editors' notes on this passage, I suddenly became aware – before I read page 30 of the General Introduction of the *Oxford Shakespeare* edition – that there was more in this passage than met the eye. I guessed that Shakespeare had a particular fishmonger in mind: some distinguished liveryman of the Worshipful Company of Fishmongers. Having already researched an unrelated theme among the Company's archives at Guildhall Library, I was confident that some significant record might be found there. I studied the transcript of the Minutes of the Fishmongers' Court of Wardens and Assistants, which date from 1595 (*Guildhall* MS st.1258/1-2).

The Fishmongers' Company, chartered in 1272, ranks fourth among the twelve 'great' City Livery Companies, famous for their closed ranks, their professed honest dealing, their charitable functions and their corporate magnificence and display, which were admired by the multitude. When Common Council received King James at his coronation, liverymen attended in their splendour of velvet gowns, satin hoods and chains of gold.

Because of their noisome trade the Fishmongers, although among the wealthiest companies, did not enjoy the social standing and respect accorded to the Mercers, Grocers and Drapers (above them in the scale) and the Goldsmiths (immediately below them). By 1603 the Fishmongers' Company had lost the reputation it should have maintained among other companies of high standing.

In the early seventeenth century dissension had been developing between the fish traders and the Company's 'metermen' or 'gagers', who inspected fish for sale and condemned it if unfit; illegal practices of mixing fresh and stale fish were rife. Other matters of concern to the Court of Assistants that managed the Company's affairs were the expense and forced loans incurred in receiving King James upon his accession and in celebrating his coronation. The renewal and maintenance of expensive livery for these occasions and the hire of a

Sir John Leman

river-barge (£5) for the annual Lord Mayor's procession were regarded by many liverymen as unnecessary extravagance. The admission of a certain outsider 'by redemption', i.e. payment, in this case, in kind, greatly shocked not only some of the more conservative Fishmongers, but also liverymen of other companies who "marvailed that this Company should bargaine and see freedomes sold . . . .". Matters came to a head in May 1604, when most of the Court of Assistants rejected their own re-election to office. The Company, under pressure from the Council of London, was promptly reconstructed under a new Prime Warden, John Leman, an 'auncient' (i.e. by patrimony) liveryman already highly regarded, even by the rebels. Dignified conduct and strict observance of the rulings of the Court were imposed by this honest man; correct behaviour among the liverymen was required; new liveries were purchased; the barge was hired, and an impressive formal dinner was held, to which leading City figures were invited, including the Lord Mayor and his Sword-bearer, a clutch of knights, among them the recently dubbed Sir Julius Caesar – a Master of the Court of Requests – and no fewer than seven Goldsmiths, whose Company, so numerously represented, gave a cachet to the occasion. Many of these events would have been perceived and noted by citizens who formed part of the *Hamlet* audience. The annual pageantry of the Lord Mayor's procession attracted great general interest.

The new Prime Warden commanded general respect. In 1605 John Leman was elected Alderman; in 1606 he served as Sheriff and in 1616, once again Prime Warden, he became Lord Mayor, the first Fishmonger to hold that office since 1590; he was knighted soon after and died in 1632. It is clear that in 1603-1604 he was seen – not by Shakespeare alone – to be an outstandingly honest man, one easily picked out among ten thousand freemen 'as the world goes', namely the commercial world of London.

These aspects of city life recall to mind the several, possibly contrived, references to Livery Companies, together with the intensity of metaphor derived from their activities.

II. ii. 497:

POLONIUS: This is too long.
HAMLET: It shall to the **barber's,** with your beard

The next direct reference to a liveryman occurs in IV. v. 42:

OPHELIA: They say the owl was a **baker's** daughter.

This too seems a contrived reference, and I offer a further textual comment on it on page 31.

Act V, Scene I contains a number of instances, the first at V. i. 29:

FIRST CLOWN: There is no ancient gentleman, but **gardeners**, ditchers and grave-makers. They hold up Adam's profession.
(The Gardeners' Company comprised market-gardeners and flower-growers, who took apprentices. Ditchers and grave-diggers were mere unskilled labourers and had no guild of any kind. The Gardeners, a guild since 1345, had recently petitioned for liveried incorporation, which was granted in 1605. A few other guild-companies were in a similar state of advancement.)

with further references at V. i. 41:

FIRST CLOWN: What is he that builds stronger than either the **mason**, the **shipwrigh**t or the **carpenter**?

The **stonemason** constructed churches, palaces and prisons; the **shipwright** crafted the bulwarks of England's defences against Spain;

the **carpenter** erected houses, barns and theatres. The last-named formed no anticlimax; perhaps First Clown made some expansive gesture encompassing the interior of the playhouse.

Another apparent reference occurs at V. i. 165:

FIRST CLOWN: A **tanner** will last you nine year . . . . . .his hide is so tanned with his trade that 'a will keep out water a great while. . . . . .
(There was no Tanners' Company; their mode of work was so stinking and repulsive that tanners were excluded from the City, settling in Bermondsey. Tanned leather could be processed (by curriers) in the City; finished products were made up and sold by **Leathersellers**. Shakespeare's father was trained as a tanner and a glover.)

I had now identified seven Companies, none bearing any apparent significance in the action of the play, that have been given attention by name, and I was prompted to look more closely into the text to find whether these instances were augmented by other names or implicit allusions.

Straightaway at I. i. 75 **Shipwrights** were mentioned by name, preceded by **Armourers**' 'implements of war' and **Founders**' 'cast of cannon'. Thereafter, instances appeared in abundance, expressed in terms closely related to the parent companies, more than fifty being reflected in strikingly vivid imagery and allusions; they are listed in Appendix II.

The one conspicuous omission from the list is the **Weavers'** Company, the oldest of them all, but of interrupted existence. Their skills engendered many metaphors in common use, so their absence needs to be accounted for. **Bottom** had already been a conspicuous success, yet although he could lord it over such artisans as a common tailor, a joiner and a bellows-mender, he was no liveryman, merely a clown with a named occupation. Perhaps the Company had taken offence at this vulgar representation of a Weaver, so Shakespeare left it out of consideration in *Hamlet*. Other companies in existence at this time were Curriers, Ironmongers, Pewterers, Plumbers, Turners, Tylers and Brickmakers, Woolmen. Shakespeare understandably found difficulty in drawing upon these for figures of rhetoric.

It may be objected that all these attributions are adventitious and merely the result of accidental associations. If so, Shakespeare's imagery is nevertheless clearly revealed as drawn from the activities of Londoners around him. But some of the examples seem so deliberately picked from contrived circumstances, for instance the Barbers, the Basket-makers, the Carpenters and the Coopers, to select the most obvious, that Shakespeare must have been aware of any casual associations and entered fully into his invented game.

Julius Caesar (first performed in 1599) opens with certain 'commoners' being rebuked for idleness. Among them are a journeyman carpenter and a cobbler, no liverymen but mere artisans, who should be distinguishable by their workaday attire and tools, in the case of the carpenter his symbolical leather apron and his rule. Like their equals in *A Midsummer Night's Dream* of a few years earlier and typical of this class in Elizabethan London, they are witty, crafty and contemptuous of petty authority, very like the grave-digger and his mate in *Hamlet* V. i, who had no guild to govern their behaviour. The invention of this scene in *Julius Caesar* may have prompted Shakespeare to develop the theme of social status and the regulation of varied personal skills and trades manifested in the livery companies.

I suggest that, having finished *Julius Caesar* and the sequence of history plays, Shakespeare may have thought of presenting a dramatic view of contemporary London, which would have been a risky venture during Elizabeth's reign; he could not, would not, attempt a new *Faerie Queene*. By the time she was out of the way he was busy with other scripts. *Hamlet* had been staged in some form or other by the end of the sixteenth century, but Shakespeare kept returning to it with revisions, amendments, additions and sometimes deletions, intending to combine aspects of London life with the historical royal Danish tragedy. The play became very digressive, very long and in its interpretation very bewildering. Always acknowledged to be flawed, *Hamlet* has challenged directors and actors alike to balance its poetic supremacy with its presentation of complex dramatic development within a questionable environment in which, for Shakespeare's private satisfaction, enigmatic allusions abound.

II. ii. 197

HAMLET: .... for the **satirical rogue** says here. . . .

Editors have struggled to identify the **satirical rogue** with Juvenal or some other author, whereas he could be more readily associated with Shakespeare himself. Indeed, Hamlet could be reading from a prominently displayed copy of the play's title-page, emphasising the alienation effect found throughout.

II. ii. 205

POLONIUS: Though this be **madness**, yet **there is method in't**
               . . . . **How pregnant sometimes his replies are!**. .
               . . . . **reason and sanity** could not so prosperously
               be delivered of

This remark is a signal to the playgoer or to the reader of the printed text that he should look out for the latent allusions to contemporaneous events and personages in the public eye. 'Fishmonger' is one; 'the satirical rogue' is another. There has been no earlier detection of this device. What may well have been recognised by a London audience of 1604 has become opaque to the modern student of the text, but clues do exist and may be perceived and deciphered. Solutions postulated here should be considered in sympathy with this premise and not be dismissed as improbable.

For Hamlet, Denmark is a prison, and the Danish Court a madhouse, from which he detaches himself with his own assumed madness. But the 'madness' dissolves into sanity (which Polonius partly recognises) when it can be applied to events and people of the contemporary London scene. Hamlet is at ease with the players from the Globe and with the grave-diggers of most un-Danish origin. But in his 'madness' he never talks nonsense; what he says relates to the sane world inhabited by the audience who, if they can perceive, will recognise it. That Shakespeare should have diverted himself in such subtlety may give us pause, but thus it remains.

I. Ii. 325

HAMLET:	What players are they?
ROSENCRANTZ:	.... **the tragedians of the city**.
HAMLET:	How chances it they travel?
ROSENCRANTZ:	I think their **inhibition** comes by the means of the late **innovation**.

On 5 May 1603 the Lord Chamberlain had closed the playhouses out of respect for James's arrival in London; they remained closed for some months on account of the plague that caused the postponement of the coronation. This was the **inhibition**.

Meanwhile, whether or not **the tragedians of the city** can be identified with The Lord Chamberlain's Men, the latter were renamed The King's Men on 19 May, with all the flummery, including the royal livery, that went with such an elevation in rank. James was a warm supporter of the theatre. Only the playhouses were closed; private performances were not affected by the Lord Chamberlain's edict.

The **innovation** was the replacement of the Tudor dynasty by that of Stuart. For Professor Jenkins **innovation** was something of a Humpty Dumpty word, which he related to Essex's rebellion of 1601. Being unsuccessful it cannot rightly be called innovatory. Any bearing on the 'tragedians of the city' seems inexplicable.

Jenkins's determined opinion, unsupported by any evidence, that *Hamlet* 'as it has come down to us' dates from 1601 has blinded him to the examination of cruxes that relate to events that occurred later than that year.

II. ii. 362

HAMLET: It is not **very strange**. For my. . . . uncle is King of Denmark, and those that would make mows at him while my father lived give twenty, forty, fifty, a hundred ducats apiece for **his picture in little**.

This would appear to be an indirect reference to the work of the miniaturists Nicholas Hilliard (1547-1619) and Isaac Oliver (c.1560-1617). Informed members of the audience would appreciate the parallel. It **is** a **very strange** observation, quite out of context yet topical. Oliver limned Queen Elizabeth in about 1592 and Anne of Denmark, James I's consort, in 1611.

II. ii. 365

HAMLET: . . . . . 'Sblood, there is something in this **more than natural, if philosophy could find it out**.

Here is another inconsequential comment, pointing to a subordinate subtlety. In I. v. 166 Hamlet tells Horatio "There are more things in heaven and earth . . . . /Than are dreamt of in your (Q2) [our (F)] **philosophy**". Some depth of thought is implied. The **philosophy** of the Ghost's existence is dramatic and essential to the plot, but the application of the term to a trivial matter of a money transaction, whether spoken in jest, irony or assumed madness, directs our attention to the latent theme. In 1603 Francis Bacon published the first part of his *On the Advancement of Learning*, in which he decried the astrological and magical explanation of natural phenomena, and proposed a more disciplined system of observation, recording and induction.

II. ii. 377

HAMLET: I am but mad **north-north-west**. When the wind is **southerly**, I know a hawk from a handsaw.

From the longitude of London Bridge and Southwark Cathedral (at that time the church of St Saviour) the bearing 22½° **west** passes

Sir Francis Bacon

Hatfield Old Palace

through no place of apparent interest until it strikes, as near as makes no matter, the Palace of **Hatfield**, of which a small range of buildings remains. Together with all other royal properties, it had been inherited by James I.

What act of madness or of folly could have troubled Hatfield? Elizabeth I had grown up there and had lived quietly in the palace during her sister Mary's reign. After her own succession she frequently hunted in its extensive forest, which she last visited in 1574. By 1592 it was 'in great decaye', although repairs were already being undertaken.

When James came to the throne the buildings had been rendered habitable, although not extensive in accommodation for people of the Court. He took a fancy to it as a hunting-lodge and a country retreat to escape from the plague that was endemic in London during the first few months of his reign, and held several courts at Hatfield in the second half of 1603, followed by others not so frequent in 1604 and 1605.

King James I

Whereas Elizabeth had been content with Greenwich, Whitehall, Richmond, and Hampton Court Palaces, all easily accessible by London's main thoroughfare, the River Thames, James's choice of Hatfield involved a tedious and difficult full-day's journey of 20 miles by road, inconvenient to the courtiers and officials whose residences were the palaces and mansions beside or very near the Thames between London and Hampton Court. The disruption and discomfort undergone by members of the Court and their own attendants became evident to those Londoners who were aware of the manner of governance of the realm. James's attitude and behaviour may well have been unreasonable; unreason was, for Horatio at least, nothing else but madness (I. iv. 73-4).

Southerly draws attention to Southwark, the location of the Globe theatre and of Shakespeare's residence in the Liberty of the Clink. The borough received balmy airs from the Kentish countryside and was for him the seat of common sense and enlightenment.

II. ii. 378

HAMLET: **I know a hawk from a handsaw**

The editor of the Oxford *Hamlet* seems satisfied that this notorious mismatch of words is a spontaneous, inconsequential remark that could well be left unexplained. But Hamlet does not resort to nonsense. Some editors elucidate by regarding **handsaw** as either an alternative to, or a typesetter's error for, **heronshaw**, which conveys some degree of sense in comparing two birds of prey in flight, although still out of context. I submit that **hawk** is the rogue word – mistaken for **hack** (a chopping tool, *OED*), which Hamlet could so well distinguish from the more precise **handsaw**. To confuse a single letter in a short word is more easily done than to fail to recognise a longer word. A **hack** and a **handsaw** are both cutting tools but used for very different purposes. The contrast between the coarse tool and the delicate implement is symbolic of Hamlet's mistrust of Rosencrantz and Guildenstern, whom he recognises as the baser tools of their regal and subtler manipulator, also engaged in the trimming trade. And at this date **hack** may already have been in colloquial use for one who has been hired.

Dr Peter Davison has suggested, however, that **hawk** may have been rightly intended in the sense of a plasterer's tool. But it is recorded in the *OED* as not used in this sense before 1700. I had already rejected it for this reason and also because of a dissimilarity between the purposes of these tools.

II. ii. 520

HAMLET: .... Good my lord, will you see the players well bestowed? Do you hear? Let them be well used, for they are **the abstract and brief chronicles of the time.** After your death you were better have a bad epitaph than their ill report while you live.

This fine-sounding phrase **"the abstract and brief chronicles"** has puzzled me. No editor or commentator finds it necessary to explain. It is one of the many examples of hendiadys in *Hamlet* (e.g. 'gross and scope', 'book and volume') so typical of the dualism in the play. It cannot be interpreted as 'chroniclers' or 'annalists'. The players do not record anything; they are records in themselves, yet able to give condemnation or praise as they perform. Shakespeare's use elsewhere of the word 'chronicle' elucidates:

(i)   CLARENCE: ... : the old folk, time's doting chronicles
(*2 Henry IV*, IV, iv)

and (ii)   HECTOR: (*to Nestor*) :Let me embrace thee, good old
chronicle,
Thou hast so long walk'd hand in hand with time:
(*Troilus and Cressida*, IV, v)

These aged survivors are in themselves evidence of times past, in a fusion of medium and message, a kind of metonymy applicable in particular to players, who present to their audience the playwright's view of life around him. They become the embodiment of the characters of his imagination, his *dramatis personae*, doubled in *Hamlet* with living worldly figures, whom Shakespeare could portray only in such disguise. Hamlet is declaring that Polonius is one of these.

III. i. 143

HAMLET: I have heard of your **paintings** too, well enough. God hath given you one face, and **you make yourselves another. You jig and amble** and you lisp. **You nickname God's creatures** and make your wantonness your ignorance.

'I have heard of . . .'; why only 'heard of'? Has Hamlet never seen any painted faces? Or was there one particular face Shakespeare had in mind that Hamlet, being Prince of Denmark, could not have set eyes on?

While addressing Ophelia with this condemnation of womankind, Hamlet is thinking of his 'queen-mother' and her guilty association with Claudius ("those that are married already, all but one, shall live."). By topical transference, the whole of this passage could relate to Queen Elizabeth I, recently deceased (24 March 1603). Her face was notoriously enamelled, and she had been an enthusiastic dancer. I have no knowledge of a lisp, yet some record may emerge.

More significantly, in November 1558, shortly after her accession, Elizabeth had declared herself to the Lords to be **"God's Creature"** who, destined by Him to reign, was yet still a frail **human being**, (*Nat. Archives PRO; SPD Elizabeth* 12/1. f7). Editors who offer a gloss on '**nickname God's creatures**' as referring to animals and even vegetables are mistaken. Elizabeth was renowned for nicknaming members of her entourage. Burghley was her 'spirit'; on 8 May 1583 she addressed a letter to him, who wished to resign office: "Sir Spirit, I doubt I do nickname you, for those of your kind, they say, have no sense." Leicester was her 'eyes', Walsingham her 'light', Whitgift her 'little black husband'. Some nicknames were cruel; the Duc d'Alençon was 'little frog', the French Ambassador de Simier 'monkey', Robert Cecil 'little man' and 'pygmy'. Such a clear reference to the Queen's *penchant* would not have been permitted on the stage during her reign, but now it became a gag. These and other examples are listed in Appendix VII.

III. ii. 108

HAMLET: (*To Polonius*) My lord, you played once i' th'university, you say?
POLONIUS: That did I, my lord, and was accounted a good actor.
HAMLET: What did you enact?
POLONIUS: I did enact **Julius Caesar**: I was killed i' th' Capitol. Brutus killed me.
HAMLET: It was a brute part of him to kill so capital a calf there.

This may be a reminder of the play of 1599, although Polonius's days at university were long past; time scales are difficult to understand in *Hamlet*. But Polonius is now perhaps enacting another, living, **Julius Caesar**, a lawyer who entertained Queen Elizabeth at his home at Mitcham in 1598, and a prominent member of the Court circle, who was knighted in May 1603. This aspect seems more impressive than Hamlet's weak punning references, made to satisfy those who were not in the know about the hidden meaning. Sir Julius was well-known among the City grandees. Perhaps Polonius was bearded and dressed up in Caesar's style. Sir Julius was the son of Elizabeth's court physician, Cesare Adelmare of Padua, whom the Queen called 'Caesar', a familiarity that prompted Adelmare's children to adopt it as a surname.

III. ii. 138

HAMLET: ....**let the devil wear black**, for I'll have a **suit of sables**

This crux has not been satisfactorily explained. I submit the following: Hamlet's words echo (a) I.ii.78-86: '. . . .**customary suits of solemn black** . . . . . . **suits of woe**', and are echoed by (b) II.ii.450:

> 'The rugged Pyrrhus, he whose **sable arms**
> **Black as his purpose**, did the night resemble'

Sir Julius Caesar

Sable is the heraldic colour **black**; the plural refers to mourning wear, and here has nothing to do with furs. **Suit** is another term for **livery**. Hamlet is in effect saying "My livery of black displays my commitment to such an evil course (the King's murder) that the Prince of Darkness, the devil himself, will 'follow suit' and adopt my livery".

III. ii. 140

HAMLET: . Then there's hope a great man's memory may outlive his life half a year. But, by'r Lady, 'a must **build churches** then, or else shall 'a suffer not thinking on, with the hobby-horse, whose epitaph is **'For O, for O, the hobby-horse is forgot!'**

In its prime meaning, a hobby-horse was a small horse, colt or pony secondly, a canvas horse-like frame borne by a performer in a morris dance, or a similar child's toy; thirdly a buffoon. But another meaning, a mistress or loose woman, is discernible in *Love's Labour's Lost* (1588), *Othello* (1603?) and *The Winter's Tale* (1611) and *could* be assigned to Hamlet's words above, yet here the phrase seems more closely associated with the man who should **build churches** or chapels, where the bodies of his family could be interred.

Most Shakespearean editors refer to the quotation as part of an untraced ballad. Several other Stuart playwrights, including Kemp, Jonson, Fletcher and Drue, are cited as quoting some variant of the phrase, e.g. **'but O, nothing but O, the hobbie-horse is forgotten.'** *(OED)*.

I question this attribution to an untraced ballad, but suggest it may have been a smart catch-phrase or refrain circulating persistently among the wits, the scribblers and playhouse-goers of the age, as a mock lament for someone who fails to get his fair, or expected, reward. The hobby-horse was the comic turn, the buffoon among the morris-dancers; he attracted much attention from the throng, but when the dancers shared out their collection from the audience, he could easily be overlooked, possibly because he was no dancer. A search among the *OED's* references might bring to light a confirmation or otherwise of this supposition.

Sir Edward Hoby

The Hoby Memorial in All Saints Church, Bisham

The **hobby-horse** may have been associated with members of the **Hoby** family, prominent in royal and diplomatic circles in the second half of the sixteenth century, for whom an ornate **burial chapel** was built at Bisham to be occupied by Sir Philip Hoby (1505-1558) and his half-brother Sir Thomas Hoby (1530-1566). The latter's elder son, **Sir Edward Hoby** (1560-1617) achieved distinction in the middle of Elizabeth's reign, partly because he was a nephew of Lord Burghley; moreover, he married the daughter of Henry Carey, Lord Hunsdon, a cousin of the Queen. He was sent on a special mission to Scotland in 1584, during which he made a favourable impression upon James VI. He became a member of several parliaments and took part in the expedition to Cadiz in 1596. He was visited at Bisham by both Elizabeth and James, the latter making him a gentleman of the privy chamber. An Oxford man, he was a scholar and a friend of William Camden. Nevertheless, he could have been a butt for the smart wits and scribblers. He was an occasional scribbler himself and in 1615 published a pamphlet under the pseudonym of 'Nick, groome of the **Hobie-stable** Reginoburgi' *(DNB)*. Does he not thereby acknowledge himself to be a hobby-horse? Although out of favour with Elizabeth for a time, he was not forgotten when James came to the throne. I fully believe that Elizabeth called him her 'hobby-horse'.

Edward's half-brother, **Sir Thomas Posthumous Hoby** (1566-1640), having married a rich lady, already thrice widowed, became involved in bitterly contested litigation in the Court of the Arches in 1601 and 1602, which became a *cause célèbre* in London. He was an object of scorn, described as "a small man, a scurvy writer, a spindle-shanked ape", but he won his case

---

III. iv. 25

HAMLET: *(drawing his sword)*: How now? A rat? Dead for a ducat, dead! *He makes a thrust through the* **arras** *and kills Polonius*

Some little time after the Earl of Essex's execution on 24 February 1601, Elizabeth's godson, Sir John Harington, paid her a visit, only to be told to "get home". In a letter to his wife he complained that " . . . . the many evil plots and designs have overcome all her Highness' sweet temper. She walks much in her Privy Chamber, and stamps with her feet at ill news, and thrusts her rusty sword at times into the **arras** in great rage". (Felix Pryor: *Elizabeth 1, Her Life in Letters,* p 127 (BL 2003).

One is left wondering whether Elizabeth's attack upon the arras was prompted by her seeing a performance of *Hamlet,* which may have been put on for her entertainment at some nobleman's house. Was she in fury and retrospect stabbing a phantom Essex, or perhaps an imaginary Southampton, unexecuted but still under sentence? Harington does not record whether she cried "How now? A rat? Dead for a ducat, dead!".

Without further examples of arras-piercing by the sword-wielding classes, one cannot imagine that it was an habitual activity of the time; it cannot be ignored as an insignificant coincidence. That Shakespeare, having also heard of the Queen's action, decided that it might be adopted with dramatic effect in disposing of Polonius, seems less likely.

Authorities agree that Shakespeare was writing *Hamlet* in about 1600, and it may have been performed in 1601, although the text was not registered at Stationers' Hall until July 1602, prior to its publication in Q1 in 1603, no more precise dates being known. In the corresponding scene in Q1 Corambis (Polonius in Q2) says "I'll shroud myself behind the arras", and exits. No further stage directions are given for Hamlet's actions; he calls out "Ay, a rat – / Dead for a ducat! Rash intruding fool, / Farewell . . ."

IV. ii. 30

HAMLET: **Hide fox,** and all after.
Exeunt

This inconsequential phrase appears for the first time in F1 but is omitted in many later editions. It could be associated with a cry after a quarry, but there is none. Following the concept that Hamlet's 'mad' sayings contain a contemporary significance, we must look for some important person or occurrence after the date of Q2 (1604-05). An immediate lead is Jonson's play *Volpone* (The Fox), first performed in 1606 and printed the following year. The rich, spiteful and cunning eponymous character was likened by some to Robert Cecil, who came to be called, among other opprobrious epithets, 'the Fox'. In 1605 he had been made Earl of Salisbury, by which title he will now be referred to, and in 1607 was promoted to the office of Lord Treasurer. In that same year he made an exchange of properties with the King, who coveted Salisbury's magnificent house of Theobalds in Hertfordshire, inherited from his father, Lord Burghley. In return for Theobalds James gave him the ancient royal palace of Hatfield, together with numerous other smaller estates, by which he became greatly enriched. Salisbury promptly planned the present house, frequently visiting the site to supervise its construction, but he never lived there; it was completed by his son.

In 1612 Salisbury was taking the waters of Bath, which he had several times visited already, but his disease was incurable; his

Sir Robert Cecil, Earl of Salisbury

condition worsened, so he decided to return to London, which he never reached, having died at Marlborough on 24 May 1612, aged 49. His body lies in Hatfield Church..

'But now in Hatfield lies the Fox,
Who stank while he lived and died of the pox.'

There is no need to look for a children's game or for an unlikely permanence given to an actor's interpolation (such as some editors propose). Shakespeare still controlled his text and never felt a need to submit to other men's emendations.

IV. v. 42

OPHELIA: They say **the owl was a baker's daughter**. Lord, we know what we are, but know not what we may be.

Such vacuous portentousness is also to be found in the enigmatic utterances of Mr F's Aunt in *Little Dorrit*, whose author thus observed this manifestation of mental derangement: "a propensity to offer remarks in a deep warning voice, which, being totally uncalled for by anything said by anybody, and traceable to no association of ideas, confounded and terrified the mind" *(Little Dorrit,* Book 1 ch. xiii) e.g. "There's mile-stones on the Dover Road!" (ch. xxiii).

This statement may have made some sense in the speaker's mind, but Dickens does not disclose it. Neither does Shakespeare in the case of Ophelia's dictum, but it is likely that he expected the audience or the reader to take in a topical understanding of the relationship between the owl and the baker, beyond a reference to an old folk tale. As yet it remains uninterpreted.

IV. v. 173

OPHELIA: It is the **false steward**, that stole his master's daughter
LAERTES: **This nothing's more than matter.**

The **false steward** will be sought in vain among the tales, ballads, and sets of verses of the time. Ophelia's remark refers to some misallied elopement, a topic of common gossip that may yet come to light, possibly in the records of courts of civil law. The reference is reinforced by Laertes's comment: '**This nothing's** more than **matter**', prompting the audience and the reader to accept the allusion.

IV. v. 184

OPHELIA: I would give you some **violets**, but they withered all when my father died.

At I. iii. 7 Laertes advises Ophelia that she should regard Hamlet as "A **violet** in the youth of primy nature". This 'violet' killed her father; until then perhaps she might still have held hopes of reconciliation. In the language of flowers 'violet' signifies modesty and innocence; its colour indicates both love and truth. Appearances are deceptive.

It seems hardly possible that Laertes's optative

> .... and from her fair and unpolluted flesh
> May **violets** spring! (V. i. 236)

may be a confused recollection of the two earlier uses of the flower's name – even on Shakespeare's part. Editors do not draw attention to the ambiguous irony of this heartfelt cry.

IV. v. 187

OPHELIA: *(sings)* For **bonny sweet Robin** is all my joy.

'For **bonny sweet Robin** is all my joy' attracts such editorial comment as "a line from an untraced ballad, 'Robin' probably referring to Robin Hood", which does not tell us much. It is more likely to refer to the priapic Robin Goodfellow (see *Percy's Reliques*), in

ROBIN
GOOD-FELLOW,
HIS MAD PRANKES AND MERRY IESTS.

Full of honest Mirth, and is a fit Medicine for Melancholy.

Printed at *London* by *Thomas Cotes*, and are to be sold by *Francis Grove*, at his shop on Snow-hill, neere the Sarazens-head. 1639.

the same bawdy strain as the exchanges between Hamlet and Ophelia in III. ii. 255-260 and her song at IV. v. 59. This may be too late an echo of Queen Elizabeth's pet-name 'Sweet Robin' for Robert Dudley, Earl of Leicester, who had died in 1588. She also addressed her cousin Sir Robert Carey, Earl of Monmouth, as 'Robin'; it was he who rushed up to Edinburgh to report her death to James VI.

IV. vii. 80
KING: . . . .Two months since
Here was a gentleman of **Normandy**.
I have seen myself, and served against, the **French**,
And they can well on horseback. . . ...
. . . .
LAERTES: A **Norman** was't?
KING: A **Norman.**
LAERTES: Upon my life, **Lamord**.
KING: The very same.
LAERTES: I know him well. He is the brooch indeed
And gem of all the nation.

IV. vii. 130

KING: We'll put on those shall praise your excellence
And set a double varnish on the fame
The **Frenchman** gave you;

The elaborate precision with which this off-stage character is presented and the background against which he is introduced presuppose a contemporary reference. Attempts have been made to identify him with an historical character. To associate him with Castiglione (1478-1529), the Italian writer of *The Courtier*, ignores entirely the emphasis upon **Norman**.

The Norman **Lamord** (Q2) [Lamourd in Q1] is described in much admiring detail. Although he does not appear on stage, he clearly represents no imaginary figure but a recognisable visitor to the Court, unidentified in editorial comment. By being thrice described as

Norman, and twice referred to as French, he is given a prominence that could have been assigned to one of the French envoys, headed by the ambassador sent over to honour the new monarch (Claudius) at his coronation. In May 1603 King Henri IV of France appointed Monsieur Philippe de Rosny, Comte de Béthune (1561-1646) as ambassador to James I. De Rosny, having already served for a spell as Henri's ambassador extraordinary to James VI at Edinburgh in 1599, was spared the usual formalities of presentation, which were delayed because of the outbreak of plague that caused the postponement of James's coronation. He was 'constantly at Court' in 1603 (*CSP Dom; Dict. de Biographie Française*).

Despite his experience as a horseman, having been captain of a company of light cavalry, de Rosny cannot be identified with Lamord, for he had no claims to Norman blood, his family having its origins in the Île de France, where he was born in the castle at Mantes-la-Jolie. Moreover, he was too old and too lofty a personage to perform such tricks as described by Claudius.

To identify the Norman among the ambassador's entourage would call for a perusal of official documents of the time, probably without success. State Papers Foreign (France) after 1600 have not been calendared; a search in the French National Archives could be unrewarding, and perhaps too demanding a task for such a problematic outcome. But I give these details in case someone may be prompted to pursue the quest.

Act V, Scene I with its manifold irrelevancies presents a number of challenging passages.

V. i. 1.

FIRST CLOWN: Is she to be buried in Christian burial when she wilfully seeks her own salvation?
SECOND CLOWN: I tell thee she is. **Therefore make her grave straight**.

Editors declare that 'straight' here means 'straight away'. I disagree. A gravedigger would not turn up to dig a grave unless he were prepared to get on immediately with the job. "Make her grave straight" says in effect "Position (not 'dig') her grave in strict alignment with the feet towards the east", a requirement for Christian burial, indicated by **'Therefore'**. Shakespeare uses **straight** mostly to mean straightway, straight away or immediately (all of which he also uses), but there are numerous instances of **straight** describing arms, backs, legs, shoulders and so on. "Make her grave **straight**" in the sense that I have proposed cannot well be expressed in any other fashion.

The expression suggests the idea of **'making'** a grave, taken up by the First Clown in line 30 and repeated in line 58, when he is overheard by Hamlet and Horatio. Hamlet in turn takes up the expression, but with ironic emphasis.

First Clown is a self-important, semi-literate buffoon, with an unduly high opinion of his own degree, from which some amusement for sophisticates in the audience may be squeezed. He calls himself, not a grave-digger (as all editors and commentators who quote from this scene refer to him) but a **grave-maker,** associating himself with gardeners, who have their own livery company, as well as with ditchers who, like grave-diggers, have none, being merely unskilled labourers on casual jobs. The lowest labouring task was that of digging. To dig a trench or a ditch or even a grave exercised no particular skill, but the term 'maker' was applicable to any worker who constructed, contrived or fabricated anything at all, from poetry and the most delicate instrument to a structure out of the coarsest of materials. The *OED* gives many examples of 'maker' combined with a head-word indicating the thing made, such as 'clock-maker' and even 'trouble-maker', but such compounds are so potentially numerous and so obvious in meaning that their inclusion is mainly academic. Both **grave-maker** and **gallows-maker** are included because it was in *Hamlet* that they were first found in print; they are not thereby warranted as standard expressions. First Clown further glorifies his job when he tells Hamlet that he is a sexton. As a **grave-maker** he was the maker of nothing; a hole in the ground is a nullity, a void. Not until it has received its incumbent can a grave be said to be 'made'.

V. i. 12, 19 and 48

FIRST CLOWN: **Argal**.

This corruption of *ergo*, Jenkins suggests, is a pun on the name of the Elizabethan logician, John **Argall**.

V. i. 14

SECOND CLOWN: Nay, but hear you, **Goodman Delver**.
FIRST CLOWN: **Give me leave.**

First Clown, with pretensions to superior knowledge and style, gives an echo of genteel condescension, **'Give me leave'**, consonant with his pleasure at being addressed as 'Goodman'. It is difficult for a modern audience to get the point of these subtle exchanges based on customs of the time and what is now obsolete linguistic usage. **'Goodman'** was a modest honorific somewhat below 'yeoman', applied to a householder, a small employer or a respectable old man: i.e. above the multitude but below the gentry. Shakespeare almost always uses it disparagingly or even contemptuously. The *OED* definition referring to this particular usage with **'Delver'** as an indication of occupation is, I am sure, inaccurate; the Second Clown is flattering his boss. 'Delver' was even at that time an archaism, I believe; a fancy word for a 'digger', echoing the medieval "When Adam delved and Eve span, who was then the gentleman?" taken up a few lines later by First Clown. Here it seems to be used as a mock occupational surname, like 'Butcher' or 'Baker', and with a capital D.

Shakespeare did use the verb 'delve' elsewhere, as in III. iv. 207 ("For 'tis the sport to have the enginer/ Hoist with his own petard, and't shall go hard/ But I will **delve** one yard below their mines/ And blow them at the moon."), but it is a usage that already has an old-fashioned flavour. In only one other play, *Cymbeline*, is it used by Shakespeare, and there in its more usual, and present, meaning of referring to research: to seek genealogical evidence and other historical information

V. i. 16

FIRST CLOWN: If the man go to this water and **drown himself**,
               . . . . he shortens not his own life.

Jenkins draws attention to the case of Sir James Hales, who **drowned himself** in 1554.

V. i. 29

FIRST CLOWN: **Come, my spade.**

First Clown demands the tool and symbol of his lowly trade as if he were a knight commanding his esquire to hand him his sword. Consider also Shirley's lines (from *Death the Leveller*, 1659) that begin "The glories of our blood and state . . .":

> "Sceptre and crown
> Must tumble down
> And in the dust be equal made
> With the poor crooked scythe and spade",

which echo a dominant theme in *Hamlet*.

First Clown addresses his mate in the familiar second person singular, 'thou' and 'thee', but Second Clown, having started with 'thee', becomes so impressed with his boss's learning that he subsequently uses the polite form 'you'.

V. i. 60

FIRST CLOWN: Get thee to **Yaughan** and fetch me a **stoup** of
               liquor.

Is this a place or a person? Many solutions to this crux have been offered, such as an alternative spelling of 'Johan', a mythical innkeeper near the Globe, or a real German or Dane in that trade. A guess that there may be a Welsh ring to it has been generally rejected, but I suggest that this is indeed its origin: a typesetter's rendering of Vaughan, a name of little significance when it first appeared in F1, published in 1623. The word may have been difficult to decipher in

Edward, Lord Zouche

the handwritten text received by the printer. Some editors omit the word altogether, dismissing it as 'corrupt'.

In December 1604 (after the publication of Q2) **Richard Vaughan** (1550?-1607), formerly Bishop of Chester, was enthroned Bishop of London in succession to the unloved Richard Bancroft, who had been made Archbishop of Canterbury after Whitgift's death. Bancroft had been an even harsher persecutor of the puritans than Whitgift himself, so his departure from London and the arrival of Vaughan, a man 'of wisdom and temperance', became an occasion for rejoicing, with barrels of beer on tap for members of the public who joined Vaughan's procession to St. Paul's Cathedral, where the precincts were largely in secular occupation. 'Get thee to Vaughan' would make good sense. Vaughan was in the Whitgift circle, having drawn up, it was said, the Lambeth Articles of Religion on Whitgift's behalf in 1594.

Long before 1600 **stoup**, like **delver**, had become an archaism (*OED*). Its use accords with First Clown's mock learning, a risible trait in many of Shakespeare's low characters, such as Bottom, Pistol, and Dogberry.

V. i. 77

HAMLET: This might be **the pate of a politician**. . . . one
          that would circumvent God, might it not?

This remark, applicable to any office-holder who broke a commandment, may have had a specific reference in 1604, difficult to pick out with certainty now, or even then. Hamlet's successive observations become more referential yet remain beyond objection because they are addressed to skulls. Members of the audiences or the readership would have had their own pet candidates.

V. i. 83

HAMLET: **My lord Such-a-one**

This hints at Edward, **Lord Zouche** (1556?-1625) (pronounced to rhyme with 'couch'), sometime President of the Marches of Wales

Sir Edward Coke

(1602) and later Governor of Dover Castle. In 1593 he was an envoy to James VI in Edinburgh and in 1598 an ambassador to Denmark; from neither assignment did he gain much credit, but he remained in the public eye, and he met with James's approval in his responsibilities in Wales and elsewhere. He was a friend of Ben Jonson, and a former pupil of Whitgift.

V. i. 96

HAMLET: Why, may not that be **the skull of a lawyer**? Where be his quiddities . . . . . This fellow might be . . . . . a great buyer of land with his statutes . . . . his fines. . . The very conveyances of his lands will scarcely lie in this box. . . .

Jenkins recognises a satirical reference to a practice among lawyers of using their legal expertise to their own advantage. He names no names, but the audience could doubtless well supply examples from their own knowledge: perhaps **Sir Edward Coke** (1562-1634), attorney-general at the time. Thomas Fuller in his *Worthies* (1662) writes of him: "Beginning on a good bottom left him by his father, marrying a wife of extraordinary wealth, having at the first a great and gainful practice. Afterwards many and profitable offices, being provident to choose good pennyworths in purchases, leading a thrifty life, living to a great age . . . . no wonder he advanced a fair estate."

Professor Jenkins's identification of these three allusions by Shakespeare (Argall, Hales and a lawyer), reveals a perception that is consistent with my own findings.

V. i. 135

HAMLET: We must speak by the card, or **equivocation will undo us**.

This theme of equivocation is given more detailed and emphatic attention in *Macbeth* (1606?) II.ii.8, wherein the PORTER, another clownish figure, quips: "Here's an equivocator, that could swear in

Sir William Dethick

both the scales against either scale; who committed treason enough for God's sake, yet could not equivocate to Heaven". Another prominent act of political equivocation may be discovered in Francis Bacon's justification to Parliament in 1603 of James's claim to the succession, in which both sides in dispute were reconciled. For these skills Bacon was rewarded with a knighthood.

V. i. 136

HAMLET: By the Lord, Horatio, **this three years I** have took note it, **the age is grown so picked** that the toe of the peasant comes so near the heel of the courtier he galls his kibe.

After 'equivocation will undo us' Hamlet digresses. **This three years** (altered from 'seven' in Q1) is so precisely expressed that it invites investigation. It cannot refer to conditions in Denmark or to any characters in the play, but it has significant bearing upon events in England between 1601 and 1604.

Ambitious wealthy social climbers, who were numerous in late Elizabethan times, could purchase the status of gentleman through a grant made by the College of Arms. Such aspirants to gentility were flooding the College with their applications – and their new money – to be granted armorial bearings. Sir William Dethick, Garter King-of-arms, did not ignore these opportunities of increasing his income from fees for researching family history, the preparation of documents and the tricking of elaborate coats of arms. Applicants were required to provide evidence of legitimate birth, religious orthodoxy, personal integrity, public service and their independence in the possession of freehold or other property. In 1596 Dethick granted a coat of arms to John Shakespeare, a somewhat doubtful candidate. In 1602, a year after his father's death, William's right of succession to this grant was challenged, but later confirmed. Dethick was accused by a colleague, Ralph Brooke, York Herald, of admitting unworthy, unqualified persons; a score of instances, including that of the player Shakespeare, were cited. Dethick's career had long been marred by disgraceful, violent behaviour and accusations of dishonesty; in January 1605 he was deprived of office.

V. i. 145

FIRST CLOWN: Young Hamlet.... he that is mad and sent into England because 'a was mad . .. . . . 'A shall recover his wits there; or, if 'a do not, 'tis no great matter there... 'Twill not be seen in him there. **There the men are as mad as he.**

This passage serves to remind the playgoer or the reader that what is madness in Denmark goes for sanity in England.

V. i. 181

HAMLET: Alas, poor **Yorick**! I knew him well.

Suggestions that **Yorick** is an invention of a Danish-sounding name may be very reasonable, yet if a convincing character to which it can be applied is to be found, he must have a **York** connection, but not of the province, the county, or the city of York, or the Dukedom of York, which was in abeyance at the time but remained present in the monarch's titles. It is possible that **York House** in The Strand may provide the clue. Since 1558 it had been the official residence of the Lord Keeper of the Great Seal, beginning with Sir Nicholas Bacon; his son Sir Francis Bacon was born there in 1561, and the Earl of Essex was examined there in 1597. What happened there in the late 1570s may still be discoverable.

V. i. 293

KING: This grave shall have a **living monument.**

The **living monument** is named in the first line of Gertrude's elegy for Ophelia, at IV. vii. 166: "There is a willow grows askant the brook".

V. ii. 33

HAMLET: I once did hold it, as our **statists** do,
         A baseness to write fair, and laboured much
         How to forget that learning.

This is no inconsequential remark spoken in 'madness', but an explanation of an action incidental to the drama, yet it contains a topical reference that would not be lost on an educated audience.

The **statists**, although literate and capable of handwriting, would dictate their letters, or draft them in rough. Penmen would copy them in 'secretary' or other official documentary hand. In such a 'base' skill statists would be untrained. For example, Archbishop Whitgift in his holograph papers resorted to a very crabbed hand with idiosyncratic spelling.

In the last quarter of the sixteenth century fair writing was becoming, for many reasons, a desirable acquirement. For instance, aristocratic and academic poets liked to present copies of their work to friends or to the objects of their affection or respect. Such scripts became even more acceptable if they were fairly written by their authors. Personal correspondence between members of the literate classes was increasing, and it became socially desirable for their writing to be legible. Although 'secretary' was commonly used, an 'Italian' style came to be favoured by many; it was easier to write and more legible. Lessons were taken from writing-masters, among whom there was great competition for pre-eminence.

The chief exponent of the skills was Peter Bales (1547-1610?), who was granted Queen Elizabeth's favour in 1575 when he presented her with a gold and crystal ring displaying, minutely written but nevertheless legible, the Creed, the Lord's Prayer and a prayer for the Queen. He was employed by Walsingham and Hatton in the exact copying of secret and intercepted letters, sometimes for forgery, similar to Hamlet's deception. These particular skills brought him involvement in the second trial of the Earl of Essex in 1601, when he gave evidence of having been approached to copy some of Essex's letters. In 1595 he addressed a calligraphic encomium in Latin to Whitgift, in whose employment he had been at one time; he applied, without success, for the post of writing-master at the School that

Whitgift founded at Croydon. His later appointment as a tutor to Henry, Prince of Wales, brought him further prominence in the eyes of the literary world.

In 1590 he published *The Writing Schoolemaster*, much of which is taken up with an *Arte of Brachygraphie*, one of the earliest attempts to construct a system of shorthand.

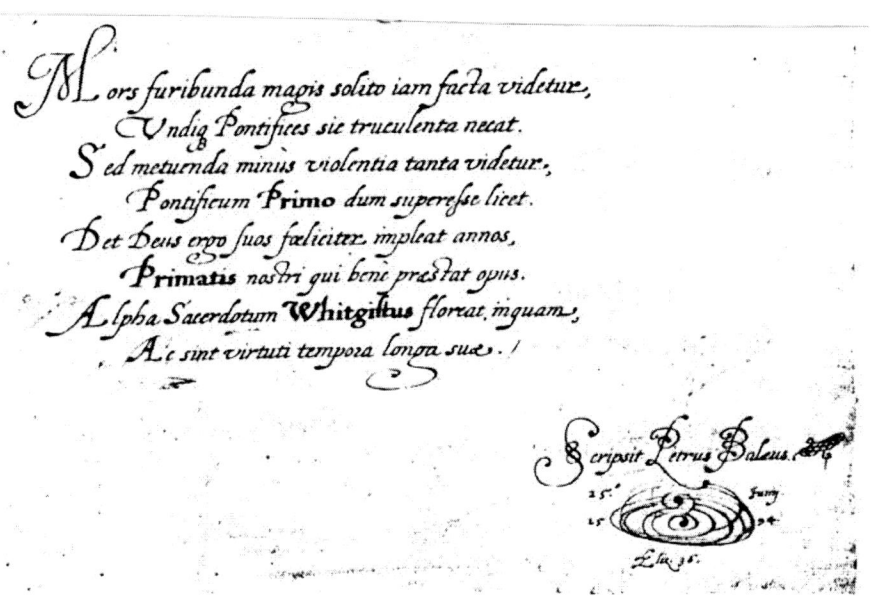

Peter Bales's enconium

Henry Prince of Wales

V. ii. 74

HAMLET: And a man's life's no more than to say '**one**'.

Dover Wilson suggests that **one** refers to a fatal rapier thrust. I believe that the blow of the executioner's axe is more in mind, catching up with Hamlet's remark fifty lines earlier: "My head should be struck off." One blow would be enough; a rapier thrust could not inflict instantaneous death. Moreover, at this point Hamlet has no knowledge of the proposed duel.

V. ii .80

Enter **Osrick**

Osrick is the subject of a vivid on-stage characterisation. His part in the play is limited to complicity with the King and Laertes in deceiving Hamlet over the foils and in umpiring the duel, but he clearly mimics some posturing fop familiar to the playgoers of 1604.

A strong candidate for the character of Osrick is the courtier Peter **Osborne** (1584-1653). His age is right, and his family background, notoriously self-seeking, is appropriate. The eldest son of Sir John Osborne (1552-1628), who was the eldest son of Peter Osborne (1521-92), he inherited jobs in the exchequer which had been held by his forebears. In 1604 he had not yet inherited 'much land and fertile', but his father was a wealthy landowner, and his mother was co-heiress to an estate, giving him expectations of '**much land**' and of being '**spacious in the possession of dirt**' (V. 11. 89-89). **Osborne** was knighted in 1611, became an MP, supported Charles I, and his son Sir John continued the family tradition of office in the exchequer.

V. ii. 374

HAMLET: .... So shall you hear
Of carnal, bloody, and unnatural acts.
Of deaths put on by cunning and forc'd cause,
And, in the upshot, purposes mistook
Fall'n on the inventors' heads.

These are but a few ingredients in a sensational story, an adventure yarn, a thriller novel or a television serial. Apart from defying the Dramatic Unities, *Hamlet* contains more narrative report than any other Shakespeare play, relating events impossible to stage.

Criminal, sinful and distasteful deeds are planned and carried out, or occur by chance; others are cited for dramatic intensity: adultery, betrayal, burial, condemnation, conspiracy, covetousness, cursing, deceit, disguise, disgrace, drowning, drunkenness, duelling, eavesdropping, envy, espionage, execution, forgery, fratricide, ghostly apparitions, harlotry, hiding, imprisonment, lust, lying, madness real and feigned, murder, mutiny, piracy, plotting, poisoning, pretence, punishment, rebellion, regicide, rejection of love and reconciliation, revenge, sedition, seduction, spite, suicide, sycophancy, theft, treason, usurpation, violence, warfare, witchcraft, wounding,. Adventures such as travel overseas, shipwreck and escape, exploits in foreign lands, visits to Hell intensify the horror of the action. These are interspersed with comic relief involving minor characters with their absurdity, jesting, ridicule, off-hand witticisms and irony, contrasting the hazards of court life with the placid station of those unburdened with responsibility.

Redeeming virtues such as ambition, compassion, constancy, filial duty and affection, prayer, pride and religious fervour are blighted in the clutch of dramatic circumstance. Even the quality of mercy is strained with thievery.

Hamlet outdoes in characterization and excitement all the popular reading matter available in the early seventeenth century such as the Holy Bible, Chaucer, Malory, other published plays, classical legends, travellers' tales, Plutarch, Boccaccio and Dante.

A work of fiction would be regarded as immoral, being untruthful and introducing imaginary characters. The Bible in particular contained vivid 'true' stories relating the deeds of violence listed above. But the astute playwright, basing his work on historical personages such as the Kings of England, Julius Caesar and Antony and Cleopatra or works already published in translation, and uncensored at that, could escape condemnation as a fantasist.

Between 1604 and 1625 the text of *Hamlet* was reprinted more often than any other of Shakespeare's plays. Readers greatly exceeded in numbers those who had only seen a stage production. The playhouses may have held many hundreds, but were not always full, and *Hamlet* was rivalled in production by many other plays. Most performances may have been presented in royal palaces, college halls, the inns of court and private houses. *Hamlet* was read, not only by those who, unable to see the play, valued it as we now get absorbed in a work of popular fiction, for its entertainment, suspense, excitement, character-drawing, with pity and terror thrown in. Although written largely in the vernacular, *Hamlet* in its felicity of expression and abundance in everyday yet vivid imagery stimulated the interest of those whose understanding of the rhetoric was uncertain.

V ii 378
HORATIO: . . . . all this can I
               Truly deliver.
FORTINBRAS: *(who has hovered faintly in the background since I .i. 95)*
               Let us haste to hear it *(why the hurry?)*
               And call the noblest to the audience.

Fortinbras seems to invite the current spectators to keep their places in the theatre, waiting for new arrivals to join them and for the curtain to rise again, with Barnardo and Francisco confronting Horatio and Marcellus in a performance that will never end: a rondeau in a continuous loop.

This, I admit, is a fanciful, extravagant and unacceptable conceit on my part, but why does Fortinbras demand such a prompt account of events leading to such overwhelming tragedy?

I. i. 19
BARNARDO: What! is Horatio there?
HORATIO: **A piece of him.**

Editors rightly point out that in the darkness Horatio could not be fully distinguishable; but a **piece** doers not quite express this idea. Which piece? A hand? his head? his body? Horatio himself could make no judgement; the viewer not the viewed would decide. His answer suggests some portion of a duality – Horatio sharing a poetic identity with Shakespeare himself.

HORATIO'S STATUS

Horatio's part in the opening scene on the castle ramparts shows him to have been a sometime soldier, temporarily re-united with some of his companions-in-arms now guarding the royal castle. (Their Italo-Roman names signify some wider region of recruitment in Europe than Denmark, whose raiding habits had been concentrated on the British Isles; and Claudius had his Switzers, too). Horatio reveals himself as having served under the late King Hamlet, possibly as a member of his bodyguard, certainly in active service against Fortinbras of Norway and Polish troops. On retirement from the Danish army, Horatio decided to study at Wittenberg, the most popular university outside Denmark for Danes and the most famous on the northern European mainland, where young Hamlet also happened to be studying. Horatio was poor, perhaps relying upon money saved during his service with the King, possibly a 'servitor' paying his way through his course, but his reply to Hamlet in I.ii.162: "Your poor servant ever," does not indicate such a status; it is as much a conventional acknowledgement of Hamlet's princely rank as is his consistent address of Hamlet as 'my lord'.

Horatio must have held King Hamlet in great respect, indeed veneration, to make his journey to attend the funeral, which had to be delayed by weeks for such distant mourners to receive the news and to put in an appearance. It seems unlikely that during the subsequent two months Horatio could have kept out of Hamlet's awareness. The hiatus is of course a dramatic requirement, and any attempt to explain it must assume both an historical and an imagined actuality in these events. Hamlet's failure to recognize Horatio immediately was due to the latter's quite unexpected appearance at the Castle, but was promptly remedied by "Sir, my good *friend*, I'll change *that* name with you."

Horatio's references to the late King's apparition are expressed in romantic terms, in contrast with Hamlet's own intimate memories of his father:

I. ii. 186

HORATIO:	I saw him once. 'A was a goodly king.
HAMLET:	'A was a man. Take him for all in all,
	I shall not look upon his like again.

211

HORATIO: I knew your father;
           [He lowers his guard, confident that Hamlet trusts him.]
           These hands are not more like.,

240

HAMLET:	His beard was grizzled, no?
HORATIO:	It was as I have seen it in his life,
	A sable silvered.

We know that "saw him once" is a meiosis. For his own good reasons Horatio does not want Hamlet to learn of his earlier close association with the King; he may not wish to reveal it for fear he should be imputed to claim some favour. Having given his reasons for being in Elsinore, Horatio was relieved that Hamlet branched off into the subject of his mother's marriage.

I.ii. 200

"Armèd at point exactly, cap-a-pe" may seem to Hamlet to be beyond the understanding of the two sentries.

226   . . . . Armed, say you? . . . . From top to toe?
            . . . . My lord, from head to foot.

As the play proceeds, Rosencrantz and Guildenstern, having revealed their obedience to Claudius's orders, are removed from Hamlet's favour, to be replaced by Horatio, as shown in III. ii. 61 onwards.

Horatio is more than Hamlet's conventional confidant, his *fidus Achates* and his eventual biographer; he has also a position in the subtext. Alone of all the characters in the play or persons referred to in it,

Horatio has no discernible status, condition or degree. As a scholar he is undefined, but his mode of expression is more poetic than that of his interlocutors in I. i and I. ii. He is impervious to the slings and arrows – and favours – of Fortune. He wears no livery, he bears no weapon, he holds no title; but he has walked with Kings – nor lost the common touch.

The idea that Horatio may have been sent by King Hamlet to watch over his son while at university should not be too readily dismissed. Whereas Rosencrantz and Guildenstern were creatures of Claudius, and Reynaldo was sent by Polonius to spy on Laertes in Paris, it is conceivable that Horatio had gone to Wittenberg to establish a friendship with Hamlet and act as an exemplar, leading him away from disreputable courses. Such a plan could account for Horatio's initial hesitancy in admitting close knowledge of King Hamlet, but Shakespeare left no other indication of the King's possible purpose. The whole rationale of the play remains shrouded in the inscrutability of its author.

Archbishop John Whitgift

ADDENDUM: WIT AND GIFTS

I. v. 40
HAMLET: O my prophetic soul! My uncle?
GHOST: Ay, that incestuous, that adulterate beast
With **witch**craft of his **wit**, with traitorous **gifts** –
O wicked **wit** and **gifts** that have the power
So to seduce – won to his shameful lust
The **will** of my most seeming-virtuous queen.

(Q2 1604, "newly printed and enlarged to be almost as much againe as it was...")

This passage, which formed the starting-point of my investigations into the latencies in *Hamlet*, has not been given the early prominence it seems to deserve, coming so soon in the play. But to the fresh reader the allusions I have perceived in it may seem too unorthodox, too extravagant, too improbable to be found in such a well-established play as *Hamlet*. If, however, my interpretations of other textual subtleties have been convincing, this one too may be acceptable.

To the present-day playgoer, to the director or producer, to the drama student or the young scholar, the name of **John Whitgift** may be quite unfamiliar, except perhaps in association with the school and hospital he founded in 1596, but to English people of the late sixteenth and early seventeenth centuries he was, as Archbishop of Canterbury, a very powerful figure indeed, greatly surpassing in importance and authority most of the courtiers and historical figures surrounding Queen Elizabeth. His modern successors as Archbishops have lost the general awe and respect that used to be accorded to the Primate of the Anglican Church. Even established historians of the Elizabethan age tend to underrate his part in affairs of state. At least one recent biographer of Queen Elizabeth I makes no mention of him at all. Later studies of him, of which there have been several, have concentrated upon his career as a churchman.

John Whitgift came to prominence as Master of Trinity College, Cambridge, in 1567. Trinity, founded in 1546 by Henry VIII, had come under Queen Elizabeth's particular patronage and interest; it was she who appointed Whitgift to the mastership on William Cecil's recommendation. Having heard him preach, she declared, "He hath a white gift indeed". Whitgift had been a Fellow of Peterhouse and Lady Margaret Professor of Divinity; he was now settled on an upward course. He ruled over a wealthy college of increasing reputation, which came to be attended by many young members of aristocratic families, including several Wards of Court entrusted to him by Cecil. Among his pupils were Robert Devereux Earl of Essex, George Clifford Earl of Cumberland, Edward Baron Zouche, the two brothers Anthony and Francis Bacon, the jurists Sir Edward Coke and Richard Cosin, and Gervase Babington, Bishop of Worcester. Many of these eminent men were in their early teens when they came under Whitgift's tuition; he gave them much personal attention, and they retained their respect and affection for him as a father figure.

In 1577 he was appointed Bishop of Worcester, in which capacity he signed Shakespeare's licence to marry. In 1583 he was translated to Canterbury, a move that was determined by the Queen, in whose trust and favour he remained until the end of her life, when he comforted her almost up to her dying breath. He subsequently crowned James I in May 1603; Whitgift died the following February.

As the senior member of Her Majesty's Privy Council, to which he was appointed in 1586, he moved in the highest circles of state, with precedence in the realm second only to the Queen herself. With her complicity he was the greatest force in the consolidation of the Church of England.

As a result of Whitgift's involvement since his Cambridge days in argument with dissident protestant factions, his name was constantly associated with disputes in liturgical matters. In 1588 he became the object of ridicule in the anonymous 'Marprelate' pamphlets, to which he responded by a rigorous search for unauthorised printing presses; he ruthlessly imprisoned the suspected authors and printers. This power dated back to his early membership of the Privy Council, which had directed him to license the publication of printed books.

THE LIFE OF THE MOST REVEREND AND RELIGIOVS PRElate *John Whitgift*, Lord Archbishop of Canterbury.

VVritten by *Sir George Paule* Knight, Comptroller of his Graces Housholde.

ROMANES. 16. 17.
Now I beseech you Brethren, marke them diligently which cause diuision and offences, contrary to the doctrine which yee haue learned, and auoide them.

LONDON:
Printed by *Thomas Snodham.*
1612.

Title page of George Paule's *Life of Whitgift*

Thereafter he became increasingly associated in the public eye with censorship of all kinds of literature and of its expression in public.

From a Privy Council meeting at Richmond Palace on 12 November 1589, which Whitgift did not attend, a letter was addressed to him in these terms: "Whereas there hath growne some inconvenience by the common plaies and interludes, playcd and exercised in and about the Cyttie of London, in that the players doe take upon them to handle in their playes certain matters of Divinitie and of State unfit to be suffred for release whereof we have thought good to appointe some persons of Judgement and Understanding to viewe and examine their plaies before they be permitted to present them publickly... we thinck it meet, and so desire your L. that some fitt persone well learned in Divinity be appointed by you to joyne with the Mr of the Revells, and one other to be nominated by the L. Mayor, and they jointly and with some spede viewe and consider of such Comedies or Tragedies, as are and shalbee publickly played by the Companions of Players in and about the Cittie of London, and they to give their allowance of suche as they shall thincke meet to be played and to forbydd the rest..."

Whitgift's involvement in censorship of stage plays was not of his own instigation but that of the other Privy Council members. The Master of the Revels (for many years Edmund Tilney) operated in the service of the Lord Chamberlain, at this time Henry Carey, first Lord Hunsdon, himself a Privy Counsellor, who was responsible for Court entertainments, including plays and masques. Among Hunsdon's own company of players, 'the Lord Chamberlain's men', was Shakespeare himself.

The Privy Council became still more active in their surveillance of plays, which in 1594 were forbidden in the City, to the great advantage of the suburbs, Southwark in particular; in 1600 plays in inn-yards were forbidden. As for printed books, although in 1593 Whitgift had personally licensed Shakespeare's *Venus and Adonis*, he decreed in 1599 the burning of several satirical and indecent works, including other Ovidian poems. In the following years the sale of engraved portraits of noblemen and others was forbidden, 'unless allowed by the Archbishop of Canterbury'. By the turn of the century Whitgift, being so closely involved in these manifold aspects of censorship, could have been regarded as the chief enemy of freedom in the publication and utterance of independent opinion and of free literary expression.

Although abstemious, Whitgift was not a man of austere, strait-laced private life. He enjoyed Court society and the company of many of his aristocratic former pupils from Trinity College, Cambridge; he visited them in their houses, where plays may have been put on as entertainment for guests. He in turn was host to his friends, and the Queen also, at Lambeth and Croydon Palaces, providing music no doubt, for he owned a fine collection of instruments for use by his own band of players. He also employed, like other magnates, a household jester – 'Ned, my Lord of Canterbury's fool' – to enliven what might otherwise have been a somewhat constrained atmosphere unrelieved by the presence of a hostess, for Whitgift was unmarried.

Whitgift's significance in history is confirmed by the fact that his *Life* by Sir George Paule, published in 1612, was the first printed biography of an Englishman written in English by a contemporary, Paule having been Comptroller of Whitgift's household.

The Archbishop of Canterbury's Palace at Lambeth was situated less than a mile and a half from the taverns and play-houses of Bankside. Members of Whitgift's household and staff could well have been frequenters. Some of them may have become personally acquainted with the players and the playwrights, even with Shakespeare himself, who would have been struck and amused by the names of Whitgift's secretary, Abraham **Hartwell**, and his steward, Christopher **Wormall**.

The resonance of **wit** and **gifts** repeated in the above quoted passage (I.v.40), with emphasis followed by **seeming-virtuous queen** may not have struck playgoers who were absorbed in listening to the Ghost's tirade, but *Hamlet* by late 1604 existed as an authentically published play, frequently reprinted and available for reading by those who enjoyed studying the text.

In 1603 a corrupt and abbreviated version of some 2000 lines was printed which seems to have been compiled from memory by some of the actors and other hands, helped perhaps by notes or primitive

The route between Lambeth and Southwark, 1574
The two circular structures off Bankside are rings for bull- and bear-baiting.
The first theatre was not built there before the late 1580's.

shorthand. The Ghost's speech quoted above is rendered in Q1 (the 'bad' quarto):

> Yea lo, that incestuous wretch wonne to his will with **gifts**
> O wicked will, and **gifts**! that have the power
> So to seduce my most seeming vertuous Queene.

'Wit' and 'witchcraft' are not there; the significant other variation is 'will'. In a contradictory manner the situation reflects a line (*1299*) from *The Rape of Lucrece* (1594):

> What **wit** sets down is blotted straight with **will**

The difference may be accounted for in various ways:
i. The text was poorly presented to the scribe (the metre is quite haphazard) or it was carelessly set up by the compositor.
ii. 'Will' suits the sense much better than 'wit' and could have been Shakespeare's first choice of word. Why would Gertrude have succumbed to the King's 'wit' – his superior intellect, which is difficult to discern – rather than to the sexual attractiveness of his person? How should his 'wit' be 'wicked'? 'Will' in Shakespearean terms and certainly in this context implies 'lust' or 'sexual drive', with greater power to seduce than 'wit'.
iii. "O wicked **will** and **gifts** . . .". The poet was too well-known as **Will** Shakespeare for this term to pass unheeded for long; it could have raised a laugh, so 'will' in its inaptness had to be replaced by a suitable word in the metre and content. The immediate conjunction of 'wit' and 'gifts' offered a splendid, almost topical, piece of word-play in 1604, when Q2 was published, and was quite safe to use, both Whitgift and Elizabeth I being out of the way by the end of February that year. 'Will' could then be transferred in the sense of 'volition' to Gertrude. 'Wit' or 'intellectual power' remained highly appropriate when associated with Whitgift, matching '**gifts**'.

Elizabeth nicknamed Whitgift her 'little black husband' because of his small stature, dark hair and beard and complexion, his devotion to her well-being, and his respect for her status.(This would be common knowledge both inside and outside Court circles.) She had been won by Whitgift's 'wit', he became her spiritual mentor and the guardian of her conscience. If Whitgift can be figured in the standard version of Q2 with the identity of Claudius, he may be regarded as the 'husband' of Queen Gertrude/Elizabeth.

'**Witch**craft of his **wit**': the Elizabethans believed that witchcraft was a potent evil, which Whitgift himself condemned in his statutes for the governance of his Hospital in Croydon, prescribing punishment for the crime of 'Witchcraft or Charminge'.

'Traitorous **gifts**', 'wicked **wit** and **gifts**': Whitgift, in common with other members of the Court, was expected to make annual gifts of gold or silver plate to the Queen on a scale more or less laid down. In return she would proffer presents in similar style, but of much smaller value. Records of such transactions, for that is what they were, show a strong balance in the Queen's favour. For example, in January 1600 Whitgift gave her gold to the value of £40, receiving in exchange a piece of silver-gilt plate weighing 45 oz., the current value being £13.10s.; other donors *pro rata*. It was Elizabeth's custom to appropriate the first fruits (the first year's rents) of an office of state or an appointed bishop, but in Whitgift's case she was less rapacious, having listened to his arguments against seizing such large sums from an impoverished church.

That Claudius should have been able to outdo King Hamlet in **wit** and **gifts** to the Queen seems surprising, but these were the honest Ghost's own words. The couple's guilty association was dominated by mutual passion, and in the King's words:

> She is so conjunctive to my life and soul
> That, as the star moves not but in his sphere,
> I could not but by her.
> (IV. vii. 14)

CONCLUSION

To what extent could any audience take heed of such symbolic codings, topical references and the veiled discrediting of institutions and persons? For that matter, we may as well ask to what extent theatre-goers appreciated the great cantata of melodious verse that was offered to them. It may have been caviare to the general, but how many of the audience at The Swan or The Globe or before a makeshift stage were aware that they were listening to immortal poetry and experienced the catch in the throat, the tingling of the scalp and the stinging of the eyes that denote its impact on our own senses?

The answer to the second question is 'none'. Shakespeare was unaware of the magnitude of his own genius as a dramatic poet. After he had given thought to the action and the characters that were to act it out, the *furor scribendi* descended upon him, driving him into a frenzy of poetic invention. But to *Hamlet* he frequently returned, adding scenes and introducing fresh dialogue and one-liners as the mood and purpose moved him.

Professor John Bayley has observed: "Shakespeare's happiest things can *seem* to come off the cuff – to the envy of Dryden and Ben Jonson – but as with all verbal art, appearances can be misleading."

Why should Shakespeare have added superfluous frills to what was already an unmanageably long dramatic work? It was also the most powerful and intense of his poetic creations, with unexampled insight into mental distress and soul-searching. As if by accident, elements of the plot had become applicable, in the critical years of 1603 and 1604, to the change in the royal succession and in the direction of religious conformity.

By 1606 Shakespeare had put *Hamlet* aside. It had been performed several times, surely not often, if ever, in its entirety, but he was not past making last minute amendments to the performing text and taking up any associative theme that presented itself. It was spontaneity and immediacy that mattered, especially at the close of a succession of performances, while the cast still had their parts in mind. A few subtle references would be recognisable by those among the audiences who were in the know. Shakespeare's fertile powers had already been deployed in the composition of several new plays, which were to form a repertoire on the London stage in which *Hamlet*, in its excessive demands upon the company of actors, no longer figured. But it was constantly revived and the frequent reprints of Q2 indicate its popularity among readers, who could enjoy the language and identify the allusions.

They went to the theatre to hear the words, much as we do, relishing the rhetoric, the grandiloquence and even the bombast, pronounced with vigour of declamation and conventional histrionic gestures. I can imagine some of the audience following the text in the Quarto open on their knees, just as I have seen foreign students with their texts at Regent's Park or music devotees with their scores at a symphony concert. The texts were mainly for private reading. Lucas Erne quotes Harry Berger's "A text which is overwritten from the standpoint of performance and the playgoer's limited perceptual capacities." (*Imaginary Audition: Shakespeare on Stage and Page*, 1989.) The books were passed round family and friends and read to bits. Some dozen copies, preserved by chance for centuries in private libraries, have survived, giving evidence of the play's popularity among the literate classes.

This deconstruction of the text should not be dismissed as a corruption of the aesthetic or literary integrity of the play. Such an elevated concept did not exist in Shakespeare's world. The perceived associations of imagery with characters, institutions and places in the England of 1604 are, I concede, mere adumbrations, hazy colourings in the atmosphere of unreality in a dramatic piece which over four hundred years has acquired the glory and reputation of holy writ. It was not so for Shakespeare; *Hamlet* was just another play which allowed him by chance to juggle with ideas and people of his time. No notion of immortality occurred to him, nor did any idea of permanent value attach itself to what he wrote for the stage. His genius had not yet been recognised.

Raymond Chandler has said: 'Alive today he would undoubtedly have written and directed motion pictures, plays and God knows what.. . . . . If some people called some of his work cheap . . . . . he wouldn't have cared a rap, because he would know that without some vulgarity there is no complete man.'

Together with a number of so far unexplained cruxes there remains the enigma of the play's symbolism. To what extent do my findings support the frequently propounded speculation that *Hamlet* may be an allegory of the condition of England at the end of the Tudor dynasty? That **Fortinbras** represents the supplanting Stuarts is not to be readily discounted. **Hamlet's father** may typify the bygone romantic and warlike England of the history plays and of catholic faith. **Hamlet** seems to stand for the disinherited generation, uncertain of its role in the world, with no clear course of action, yet constantly seeking justification of its own inconsistent impulses, without much understanding of the interests and motives of ordinary humanity. If so, **Gertrude/Elizabeth** is the Tudor monarch, married – even in doubly figurative terms – to the usurping protestant faith (**Claudius/Whitgift**). **Ophelia** is the innocent incarnation of the romantic rural and floral England of *As You Like It*; **Laertes** displays the rash and vindictive spirit of an English adventurer. Their father, **Polonius**, is the spying, meddling Privy Councillor, at odds with all who vainly look to him for wise direction. **Horatio**, confidant of obscure origin and poetically gifted narrator, may be identified with **Shakespeare** himself, a hypothesis that could lead to further speculation.

Martin Jarvis as Hamlet (left) and Roger, Lord Freeman as Laertes (right) in a production of *Hamlet* at Whitgift School 1958

APPENDIX I

Imagery associated with Livery Companies

1. Apothecaries, Society of

III. ii. 315	For me to put him to his purgation . . .
III. iii. 97	This physic but prolongs thy sickly days.
III. iv. 146	Lay not that flattering unction to your soul,
IV. iii. 9	Diseases desperate grown By desperate appliance are relieved,
IV. vii. 142	Where it draws blood no cataplasm so rare, Collected from all simples that have virtue
V. ii. 308	No medicine in the world can do thee good.

2. Armourers

I. i. 74	. . . . foreign mart for instruments of war,
I. ii. 200	Armèd at point exactly, cap-a-pe,
I. iv. 52	. . . . thou, dead corse, again in complete steel,
II. ii. 487	. . . . never did the Cyclops' hammers fall On Mars's armour, forged for proof eterne,

3. Bakers (see also Cooks)

III. iii. 80	'A took my father grossly, full of bread,
IV. v. 42	They say the owl was a baker's daughter.

4. Barbers

II. ii. 497   It shall to the barber's, with your beard.

5. Basket-makers

III. iv. 195   Unpeg the basket on the house's top.

6. Blacksmiths

I. iii. 63   Those friends thou hast. . . .
                Grapple them unto thy soul with hoops of steel.

III. ii. 93   . . . . my imaginations are as foul
                As Vulcan's stithy.

III. iii. 25   . . . . we will fetters put about this fear,

7. Bowyers (see also **Fletchers**)

IV. vii. 21   . . . . my arrows,
                Too slightly timbered for so loud a wind,
                Would have reverted to my bow again,

8. Brasiers

III. iv. 36   . . . . let me wring your heart. . . .
                If damnèd custom have not brassed it so

9. Brewers

III. ii. 49   'Your beer is sour,
                [only in Q1, probably removed for Q2 because of
                its triviality or lack of respect for Brewers].

10. Broderers

II. i. 77   . . as I was sewing in my closet,
            [Ophelia had her embroidery or tapestry; she had
            no need to sew or repair garments.]

11. Butchers

II. ii. 511	When she saw Pyrrhus with malicious sport In mincing with his sword her husband's limbs,
II. ii. 576	I should ha' fatted all the region kites With this slave's offal.

12. Carpenters

II. ii. 377	When the wind is southerly, I know a hack from a handsaw.
V. i. 41	What is he that builds stronger than either the mason, the shipwright or the carpenter?

13. Clothworkers (see also **Merchant Taylors**)

I. i. 167	But look, the morn in russet mantle clad
I. ii. 77	'Tis not alone my inky cloak, good mother, Nor customary suits of solemn black,
I. iii. 70	Costly thy habit as thy purse can buy, But not expressed in fancy;

14. Cooks (see also **Bakers**)

I. i. 98	Sharked up a list of lawless resolutes For food and diet to some enterprise That hath a stomach in't;
I. ii. 143	Why, she would hang on him As if increase of appetite had grown By what it fed on.
I. ii. 180	The funeral baked meats Did coldly furnish forth the marriage tables,
II. ii. 440	. . . . no sallets in the lines to make the matter matter savoury,

15. Coopers

V. i. 207 . . . . why of that loam whereto he was converted, might they not stop a beer-barrel?

16. Cordwainers

I. ii. 147 A little month, or ere those shoes were old
With which she followed my poor father's body

II. ii. 230 Nor the soles of her *(Fortune's)* shoe?

III. ii. 285 . . . . two Provincial roses on my razed shoes,

17. Cutlers

III. i. 75 When he himself might his quietus make
With a bare bodkin?

III. ii. 403 I will speak daggers to her, but use none.

18. Distillers

I. ii. 204 . . . . distilled
Almost to jelly with the act of fear,
[The Distillers and the Horners did not receive their Charters until 1638; the Distillers probably, like the Horners certainly, already existed from an earlier date in corporate form.]

19. Drapers

II. ii. 506 . . . . for a robe
About her lank and all o'er-teemed loins,
A blanket in the alarm of fear caught up –

20. Dyers

I. iii. 127 Do not believe his vows. For they are brokers,
Not of that dye which their investments show,

21. Fishmongers

| II. ii. 173 | POLONIUS: | Do you know me, my lord? |
| | HAMLET: | Excellent well. You are a fishmonger. |

22. Fletchers (see also **Bowyers**)

| III. i. 58 | The slings and arrows of outrageous fortune |
| IV. vii. 21 | .... my arrows,
 Too slightly timbered for so loud a wind,
 Would have reverted to my bow again, |

23. Founders

| I. i. 73 | ..... why such daily cast of brazen cannon |

24. Fruiterers

| II. ii. 52 | My news shall be the fruit to that great feast. |
| III. ii. 200 | Which now, like fruit unripe, sticks on the tree, |

25. Gardeners

I. ii. 135	.... 'tis an unweeded garden That grows to seed.
I. iii. 39	The canker galls the infants of the spring Too oft before their buttons be disclosed.
III. iv. 152	.... do not spread the compost on the weeds To make them ranker.
V. i. 29	There is no ancient gentlemen but gardeners,

26. Girdlers

| V. ii. 147 | .... six French rapiers and poniards, with their <br> assigns, as girdle, hangers and so. |

27. Glaziers

III. ii. 21	. . . . to hold, as 'twere, the mirror up to nature,
III. iv. 20	You go not till I set you up a glass Where you may see the inmost part of you.

28. Goldsmiths

II. ii. 427	Pray God your voice, like a piece of uncurrent gold, be not cracked within the ring.
III. iii. 58	Offence's gilded hand may shove by justice;
IV. i. 25	. . . . like some ore Among a mineral of metals base, Shows itself pure.
IV. vii. 93	. . . . He is the brooch indeed And gem of all the nation.

29. Grocers

III. i. 47	. . . . with devotion's visage And pious action we do sugar o'er The devil himself.
III. ii. 70	. . . . let the candied tongue lick absurd pomp,

30. Haberdashers

I. iv. 65	I do not set my life at a pin's fee.
II. i. 78	Lord Hamlet, with his doublet all unbraced, No hat upon his head, his stockings fouled, Ungartered, and down-gyvèd to his ankle,
II. ii. 229	On Fortune's cap we are not the very button.
IV. vii. 76	A very riband in the cap of youth,
V. ii. 94	Put your bonnet to his right use. 'Tis for the head.

31. Horners

I. v. 98	Yea, from the table of my memory I'll wipe away all trivial fond records,
I. v. 107	My tables – meet it is I set it down
II. ii. 136	If I had played the desk or table-book, ['table', 'tables', 'table-book' all relate to a small personal note-book comprising a pair hard covers, usually of ivory or horn, enclosing pieces of parchment, paper or thin horn, upon which memoranda could be written, perhaps in lead-point or with a graphite stick, whose marks were erasable. (This is pure conjecture, no examples having survived, but surely an improvement on the waxen tablet.)]

32. Innholders

I. v. 151	You hear this fellow in the cellarage.

33. Joiners

I. ii. 19	Or thinking by our late dear brother's death Our state to be disjoint and out of frame,

34. Leathersellers

I. iii. 70	Costly thy habit as thy purse can buy,

35. Loriners

IV. iv. 32	How all occasions do inform against me And spur my dull revenge!

36. Masons

I. iv. 48	. . . . the sepulchre Wherein we saw thee quietly interred Hath oped his ponderous and marble jaws To cast thee up again.

V. i. 41	What is he that builds stronger than either the mason, the shipwright, or the carpenter?

37. Mercers

II. ii. 163	Be you and I behind an arras then.

38. Merchant Taylors (see Clothworkers)

I. ii. 77	'Tis not alone my inky cloak, good mother, Nor customary suits of solemn black,
I. iii. 70	Costly thy habit as thy purse can buy, But not expressed in fancy; rich, not gaudy; For the apparel oft proclaims the man,

39. Musicians

III. i. 157	That sucked the honey of his music vows,
III. ii. 80	. . . . they are not a pipe for Fortune's finger To sound what stop she please.
III.ii.365	Govern the ventages with your finger and thumb; give it breath with your mouth; and it will discourse most eloquent music

40. Painter-Stainers

II. i. 90	He falls to such perusal of my face As 'a would draw it.
II. ii. 364	. . . . give. . . . a hundred ducats apiece for his picture in little.
II. ii. 479	So as a painted tyrant Pyrrhus stood,
III. iv. 54	Look here upon this picture, and on this, The counterfeit presentment of two brothers.
IV. vii. 131	. . . . set a double varnish on the fame The Frenchman gave you;

41. Paviors

I. iii. 50   Himself the primrose path of dalliance treads

42. Plaisterers

III. i. 51   The harlot's cheek, beautied with plastering art,

43. Poulters

III. ii. 103   I eat the air, promise-crammed. You cannot feed capons so.

IV. iii. 21   We fat all creatures else to fat us, and we fat ourselves for maggots .

44. Saddlers

IV. vii. 84   . . . . He grew unto his seat
And to such wondrous doing brought his horse

45. Salters

I. ii. 154   Ere yet the salt of most unrighteous tears
Had left the flushing in her gallèd eyes,

III. ii. 165   Neptune's salt wash and Tellus' orbèd ground,

IV. v. 157   . . . . Tears seven times salt
Burn out the sense and virtue of mine eye!

46. Scriveners

V. i. 107   . . . . than the length and breadth of a pair of indentures?

V. ii. 33   I once did hold it, as our statists do,
A baseness to write fair.

47. Shipwrights

I. i. 75   Why such impress of shipwrights, whose sore task
Does not divide the Sunday from the week.

V. i. 41   What is he that builds stronger than either the mason, the shipwright, or the carpenter?

48. Skinners

V. i. 112   Is not parchment made of sheep-skins?
Ay, my lord, and of calves' skins too.

49. Stationers

I. v. 100   All saws of books, all forms, all pressures past . .
. . ..
Within the book and volume of my brain.

III. i. 44   . . . . Read on this book
That show of such an exercise may colour
Your loneliness.

50. Tallow-chandlers

IV. vii. 114   There lives within the very flame of love
A kind of wick or snuff that will abate it,

51. Upholders

I. v. 82   Let not the royal bed of Denmark be
A couch for luxury and damned incest.

II. ii. 422   . . . . thy face is valanced since I saw thee last.

52. Vintners

I. iv. 10   . . . . s he drains his draughts of Rhenish down

V. i. 176   'A poured a flagon of Rhenish on my head once.

53. Wax-chandlers

III. iv. 85   To flaming youth let virtue be as wax
And melt in her own fire.

54. Wheelwrights

II. ii. 493   Break all the spokes and fellies from her
                              (*Fortune's*) wheel
            And bowl the round nave down the hill of
                                        heaven,

APPENDIX II

Livery

The theme of **Livery**, not so much in connection with the City Companies, but in its symbolic meanings of an inherited disposition or an acquired guise, is played upon in these three instances from Q2 only::

I.iv.30

    HAMLET: . . . . – that these men,
                            Carrying, I say, the stamp of one defect,
                            Being **nature's livery** or fortune's star,

I.iv. 162
    HAMLET   That monster custom, ...
                            . . . .
                            He likewise gives a **frock or livery**
                            That aptly is put on.

IV. vii. 77
    KING: . . . . for youth no less becomes
                            The light and careless livery that it wears
                            Than settled age his sables and his weeds,

These passages may have been omitted from the Folio because of their irrelevancy or, which seems to me more likely, because they all include derogatory references to the uniform of respectability among City Freemen and the King's Players.

APPENDIX III

Heraldry

Shakespeare derived his own status of gentleman from his father, whose grant of arms defined the rank of his descendants. As a mere 'player', however successful, he would have found difficulty in pursuing a claim for a grant. Now, secure in his inherited, elevated condition, he was disposed to draw confidently upon heraldic themes in his dramatic imagery;

I. i. 87	.... a sealed compact Well ratified by law and heraldry,
I. v. 21	But this eternal blazon must not be To ears of flesh and blood.
II. ii. 450	'The rugged Pyrrhus, he whose sable arms, Black as his purpose, did the night resemble . . . . Hath now this dread and black complexion smeared With heraldry more dismal. Head to foot Now is he total gules, horridly tricked
III. iv. 59	A station like the herald Mercury
IV. v. 215	No trophy, sword, nor hatchment o'er his bones,
V. i. 29	

FIRST CLOWN: There is no ancient gentlemen but gardeners, ditchers, and grave-makers. They hold up Adam's profession.
SECOND CLOWN: Was he a gentleman?
FIRST CLOWN: 'A was the first that ever bore arms.

The description of Shakespeare's coat of arms is, in plain terms, 'a gold shield in which a bend sable contains a gold spear with its steel tip represented inm silver; for crest a flacon with silver wings displayed, standing on a wreath and supporting a gold spear, steeled as before.' He 'displayed' wings indicate a shaking of the spear. NON SANZ DROICT seems to be a motto, which was not used in any contemporary display of the arms.

APPENDIX IV

Weaponry

A full range of weaponry is found in *Hamlet,* both on and off the stage. At the head come the **cannon** (I. i. 73 and I. ii. 126), the **murdering-piece** (IV. v. 96), and the engineer's **petard** (III. iv. 208), all explosive devices in set-up emplacements. The remainder are personal arms, borne according to rank, and many figure in armorial bearings:

I. ii. 204	the King-marshal's **truncheon,** sceptre or baton
II. ii. 467	the warrior-prince's **sword**
IV. i. 10	the nobleman's **rapier**
II. ii. 320	the knight's **foil**
III. ii. 404	the gentleman's **poniard** or **dagger**
III. i. 58 & IV. vii. 21	the yeoman/bowman's **arrow**
I. i. 141	the foot-soldier's **partisan**
III. i. 58	the obsolete **sling**
V. i. 89	the sexton's **spade**, used by the grave-digger to batter a skull
V. i. 56	the vagabond's **cudgel**
V. i. 77	Even **Cain's jaw-bone** of an ass gets a mention
II. ii. 355	Such unwarlike people as poets and players resort to **fisticuffs.**
II. ii. 342	And even rapier-bearers are afraid of **goose-quills.**

III. i. 76   A suicide, of whatever condition, could resort to
               a **bare bodkin**.

Yet all these weapons are subordinate to (a) the headsman's **axe**, the privileged and instantaneous means of execution accorded to kings, queens and nobles:

V. ii. 24

HAMLET: No, not to stay the grinding of the **axe**,
            My head should be struck off.

V. ii. 74

HAMLET: And a man's life's no more than to say **'one'**.

and (b) the hangman's **noose**, the base fate of the common miscreant, who endures prolonged suffering before his death:

V. i. 46

FIRST CLOWN: The **gallows** does well. . . It does well to those that do
             ill.

Many of these items seem to be felicitously introduced for the purpose of imagery alone, to fill gaps in the schedule, as it were. Noticeably absent is the jousting-**spear,** Shakespeare's own heraldic device, contained within his name and printed on the play-sheets and the title-pages of some of his published works.

APPENDIX V

Social Status

An important underlying theme is that of social position, rank, condition and degree, which were firmly ordained by birth but which could be elevated through merit (nature's livery), favour or the wheel of Fortune, which could spin either way: to success or to disaster. The vagaries of Fortune's wheel receive much attention in the play: II. ii. 228, III. i. 58, III. ii. 80, III. iv. 34, IV. iv, 52, V. ii. 382. Destiny in the Calvinist sense does not come into the reckoning. Spiritual and bodily existence after death was imagined with horror and despair. Hamlet calls upon his 'fate' because it is part of his inheritance;

> ....My fate cries out
> And makes each petty artere in this body
> As hardy as the Nemean lion's nerve."

Even as his fate was determined, malicious Fortune intervened;

> The time is out of joint. O cursed spite
> That ever I was born to set it right."

The whole range of social status, so important in Elizabeth's competitive times because of the possibilities of advancement in the middling grades at least, is displayed in *Hamlet* as if to emphasise the differences and to comment on them. Modes of address are pointedly directed and even defined:

V.i. 209	**Imperious Caesar,** dead and turned to clay,
IV. v. 21	Where is the **beauteous majesty** of Denmark?
IV. v. 125	There's such **divinity** doth hedge a **king**
II. ii. 65	It was against **your highness** (Voltimand to Claudius)

II. ii.86	**My liege** (Polonius to Claudius).
II. ii. 141	Lord Hamlet is a **prince**, out of thy star. (Polonius to Ophelia)
II. ii. 213	**My honourable lord** (Polonius to Hamlet).
II. ii. 541	Follow **that lord,** and look you mock him not. (Hamlet to First Player, referring to Polonius).
V. i. 220	Laertes, a very **noble** youth (being the son of Polonius).
II. ii. 320	the **adventurous knight** shall use his foil and target.
V .ii. 107	an **absolute gentleman,** . . . the card or calendar of gentry. (Osrick of Laertes).
II. ii. 369	**Gentlemen,** you are welcome to Elsinore. (Hamlet to Rosencrantz and Guildenstern).
II. ii. 420	You are welcome, **masters**, welcome, all. (Hamlet to the players)

['Masters' may seem an unduly elevated degree, but these are senior members of the King's Company, who wear the royal livery, a mark of minor gentry. Individuals would be addressed as 'Master So - and - so'; Hamlet also calls them 'friends', but never 'gentlemen'. He welcomes Rosencrantz and Guildenstern with "My excellent good friends" and "Good lads" as well as "gentlemen". Polonius wants to use the players "according to their desert", i.e. their condition, which to him remains servile. Hamlet rebukes him, using such elevated terms as honour, dignity, merit and bounty.]

V. ii. 36	It did me **yeoman's** service.

[It would be unusual to associate writing-skills specifically with a yeoman, which term was often applied to an upper servant in a royal or noble household, ranking below a squire or a gentleman *(OED)*. A rustic yeoman could be a small landowner, but in this context a reliable deputy or a petty official, on the fringe of literacy and able to keep neat records, is to be imagined.]

III. ii. 33	I have thought some of Nature's **journeymen** had made men, [unskilled craftsmen not yet admitted to livery].
V. i. 14	.... **Goodman** Delver [see also page 38]
I. i. 78	... this sweaty haste Doth make the night joint-**labourer** with the day? [an unskilled manual worker].
V. i. 135	How absolute the **knave** is! [Hamlet of First Clown: a menial, one of low condition.]
II. ii. 547	O, what a **rogue and peasant slave** am I! (a mere serf.)
V. i. 137	... the age is grown so picked that the toe of the **peasant** comes so near the heel of the **courtier** he galls his kibe.
IV. v. 103	.... Laertes, in a riotous head, O'erbears your officers. The **rabble** call him **lord**,
II. ii. 272	**Beggar** that I am, I am even poor in thanks.

[Beggars had to provide themselves with licences, without which they would go to Bridewell, the lodging of the lowest class of all – the debtor's prison.]

0IV. iii. 20 ...	... Your **worm** is your only **emperor** for diet. ... Your fat **king** and your lean **beggar** is but variable service That's the end. (The wheel turns full circle.]

The matter of degree is always present, with emphasis on the degradation that results from base associations:

V. ii. 60	'Tis dangerous when the **baser nature** comes Between the pass and fell incensèd points Of mighty opposites.

[Rosencrantz and Guildenstern are sacrificed in the contest between Hamlet and Claudius.]

V. ii. 33   I once did hold it, as our statists do,
            A baseness to write fair,

[Such skill implied an acquirement, a mere manual practice, without 'merit'.]

V. i. 199   To what **base** uses we may return, Horatio! Why may not imagination trace the noble dust of Alexander till 'a find it stopping a bunghole?

[The ultimate degradation that has become Hamlet's *idée fixe*.]

APPENDIX VI

Other Imagery

The imagery in *Hamlet* has already received great attention and profound commentary by other hands; its vivid and sensual strength is sometimes based on sporting or other worthy activities but most often on desire, corruption, evil and debauchery. Another prominent aspect is the use of symbols from the world of nature, animals and flowers, and of parts of the human body, reflective of human character and propensities. The animal kingdom has its own order of precedence and degree, in parallel with mankind. Man is 'the paragon of animals'; the Nemean lion is at the head of the sub-human species, with the maggot at its base, yet the eventual consumer of all above it.

In addition to the Court, the College of Arms, and the City Livery Companies, many of the national and City institutions receive attention. They include the Church, the Royal Exchange, the judiciary, the Inns of Court, the stage, the soldiery and, although least in reputation, not so in frequency of mention: prisons and the stews.

Animals are also elements in heraldry; perhaps research has already been done on their representation in armorial bearings of the time, which may include such beasts as harts, lions, pelicans, porcupines, serpents and so on, that are also used in the play's imagery.

APPENDIX VII

Some Nicknames used by Queen Elizabeth I

Cesare Adelmare:	Caesar
Duc d'Anjou (earlier d'Alençon)	Froggy, my little frog, etc.
Charles Blount, Lord Mountjoy:	mistress kitchenmaid (after he described himself as 'a scullion'), my faithful George.
Francis Bacon:(as a child):	my young keeper, my watch candle
Henry Carey, Lord Hunsdon:	my Harry
Robert Carey, Earl of Monmouth (her cousin or, possibly, half-brother):	Robin
Robert Cecil:	little man, pygmy, elf
William Cecil:	alpha and omega; my spirit, sprite, eremite of Theobalds.
Dr John Dee:	philosopher
Robert Dudley, Earl of Leicester:	gypsy, two eyes, sweet Robin
Dr Richard Fox, Bishop of Ely:	proud prelate
Sir John Harington:	boy Jack, that saucy poet my godson

Sir Christopher Hatton: mutton, bell-wether, pecora campi

Lady Norris, mother of Sir John: mine own crow

Sir Walter Raleigh: water, pug, my virtuous lover, fish, goose, shepherd of the ocean

Jean de Simier, French Ambassador: ape, monkey

Sir Francis Walsingham: my light, my moon, Moor

John Whitgift, Archbishop of Canterbury: my little black husband

An unknown follower of d'Anjou: the Monk

SELECT BIBLIOGRAPHY

Cecil, David: *The Cecils of Hatfield House* (1973)

Cowden Clarke, Mrs: *Complete Concordance to Shakespeare* (1874)

Patrick Collinson: "William Shakespeare's Religious Inheritance" in *Elizabethans* (2003)

H.M. Colvin (ed.): The History of the King's Works, Vol. IV, 1485-1660 (Part II) (1982)

Complete Peerage

Dictionary of National Biography

Michael Dobson and Sir Stanley Wells (eds): *Oxford Companion to Shakespeare* (2000)

Lukas Erne: *Shakespeare as Literary Dramatist* (2003)

F E. Halliday: *A Shakespeare Companion 1564-1964* (1964)

G. B. Harrison (ed.): *The Letters of Queen Elizabeth* (1935)

Valerie Hope, Clive Birch and Gilbert Torry: *The Freedom:* the past and present of the Livery, Guilds and City of London (1982)

John Jump (ed.): *Hamlet, a Casebook* (1968)

Christopher Lee: *1603, The Death of Elizabeth and the Birth of the Stuart Era* (2003)

Peter Levi: *The Life and Times of William Shakespeare* (1988)

Joanna Moody (ed.): *The Private Life of an Elizabethan Lady, the Diary of Lady Margaret Hoby, 1599-1605,* (1999)

Oxford English Dictionary

Liza Picard: *Elizabeth's London* (2003)

Felix Pryor: *Elizabeth 1, her life in Letters* (2003)

S. Schoenbaum: *William Shakespeare, a Compact Documentary Life* (1987)

Ben Weinreb and Christopher Hibbert (eds.): *The London Encyclopaedia* (1983)

J. Dover Wilson: *What Happens in Hamlet* (1935)

INDEX OF PERSONS

(Numbers in italics indicate illustrations)

Adelmare, Cesare, 31, 98
Alençon, Duc d', 30, 98
Anjou, Duc d', 98
Anne of Denmark, 15, 24
Armstrong, Archibald, 15
Argall, John, 45, 50

Babington, Gervase, Bishop of Worcester, 66
Bacon, Anthony, 66
Bacon, Sir Francis, 24, *25*, 52, 53, 66, 98
Bacon, Sir Nicholas, 53
Bales, Peter, 54, *55*
Bancroft, Richard, Archbishop of Canterbury, 48
Bayley, Professor John, 73
Berger, Harry, 74
Blount, Charles, Lord Mountjoy, 98
Brooke, Ralph, 52

Caesar, Sir Julius, 18, 31, *32*
Camden, William, 35
Carey, Henry, First Lord Hunsdon, 35, 68, 98
Carey, Robert, Earl of Monmouth, 42, 98
Castiglione, 42
Cecil, Robert, Earl of Salisbury, 12, 30, 37, *38*, 39, 98
Cecil, William, Lord Burghley, 12, 30, 35, 37, 66, 98
Chandler, Raymond, 74
Charles I, King, 57
Clifford, George, Earl of Cumberland, 66
Coke, Sir Edward, *49*, 50, 66
Collinson, Professor Patrick, 11
Cosin, Richard, 66

Davidson, Dr Peter, 29
Dee, Dr John, 98

Dethick,. Sir William, *51*, 52-3
Devereux, Robert, Earl of Essex, 23, 36, 53, 54, 66
Dickens, Charles, 39
Drue, 33
Dryden, John, 73
Dudley, Robert, Earl of Leicester, 30, 42, 98

Elizabeth I, Queen, 12, 15, 23, 24, 26, 30, 31, 35, 36, 42, 54, 63, 65, 66, 70-1, 75, 93, 98
Erne, Lucas, 74

Fletcher, John, 33
Fox, Dr Richard, Bishop of Ely, 98
Freeman, Roger, Lord Freeman, *76*
Fuller, Thomas, 50

Goodfellow, Robin, 40, *41*

Hales, Sir James, 45, 50
Harington, Sir John, 36, 98
Hartwell, Abraham, 69
Hatcliffe, William, 11
Hatton, Sir Christopher, 54, 99
Henri IV, King of France, 43
Henry VIII, King, 66
Henry, Prince of Wales, 55, *56*
Herbert, William, Earl of Pembroke, 11
Hilliard, Nicholas, 24
Hoby, Sir Edward, *34*, 35-6
Hoby, Sir Philip, 35
Hoby, Sir Thomas, 35
Hoby, Sir Thomas Posthumous, 36
Hood, Robin, 40
Hotson, Professor Leslie, 11

James VI and I, King, 11, 15, 17, 23, 24, 26, *27*, 28, 35, 36, 37, 42, 43, 50, 65
Jarvis, Martin, *76*
Jenkins, Professor Harold, 13, 23, 45, 46, 50

Jonson, Ben, 11, 33, 37, 50, 73
Juvenal, 22

Kemp, William, 33

Leman, Sir John, *17*, 18
Lord Mayor of London, 18, 67

Mary I, Queen, 26

Ned, 'my Lord of Canterbury's Fool', 69
Norris, Lady, 99
Norris, Sir John, 99

Oliver, Isaac, 24
Osborne, Sir John, 57
Osborne, Sir Peter, 57
Osborne, Peter, 57

Paule, Sir George, 67

Raleigh, Sir Walter, 99
Rosny, Philippe de, Comte de Béthune, 43
Rowse, Dr A.L., 11

Shakespeare, John, 20, 52, 89
Shirley, James, 46
Simier, Jean de, 30, 99

Tilney, Edmund, 68

Vaughan, Richard, Bishop of London, 48

Walsingham, Sir Francis, 30, 54, 99
Whitgift, John, Archbishop of Canterbury, 30, 48, 50, 54, 63-71, *64*, 75, 99
Wilson, Professor Dover, 11, 13, 57
Wormall, Christopher, 69
Wriothesley, Henry, Earl of Southampton, 11, 36

Zouche, Edward, Lord Zouche, *47*, 48-9, 65

INDEX OF PLACE-NAMES

Athens, 12

Bath, 37
Bisham, Berks, 35

Cadiz, 35
Cambridge, 66:
  Peterhouse, 66
  Trinity College, 66, 69
Canterbury, 66
Chester, 48
Croydon, 55, 69, 71
  Whitgift School, 55, 65, 72, 76

Denmark, 12, 22, 24, 30, 50, 52, 53, 61
Dover, 39, 50

Edinburgh, 42, 43, 50
Elsinore, 61, 62
England, 12, 13, 19, 53, 74, 75

France:
  Île de France, 43
  Normandy, 42

Greenwich, 28

Hampton Court, 28
Hatfield, 26, *26*, 37, 39

Illyria, 12

London and Environs, 11, 23
  Bermondsey, 20
  City, 16, 18, 20, 31, 68, 97
  College of Arms, 52, 97

London and Environs (cont.)
  Court of the Arches, 36
  Guildhall, 17
  Inns of Court, 97
  Lambeth, 68, 69, *70*
  London Bridge, 24
  Regent's Park, 74
  Royal Exchange, 97
  Southwark:, 28, *70*
    Bankside, 69
    Globe Theatre, 22, 28, 46, 73
    Liberty of the Clink, 268   St Saviour's Church, 24
    Southwark Cathedral, 24
    Swan Theatre, 73
  St Paul's Cathedral, 48
  Stationers' Hall, 37
  Thames, River, 28
  Whitehall, 28
  York House, 53

Mitcham, 31

Padua, 31

Richmond, 28, 67

Stratford-upon-Avon, 11

Wales, 48
Worcester, 65

York, 53

INDEX OF ANNOTATIONS

I. i. 19	Horatio – A piece of him	60
I. i. 75	Shipwrights	20
I. i. 82	Fortinbras	15
I. ii. 186	I saw him once. 'A was a goodly king	61
I. iii. 7	violet of youth	40
I. v. 44	Wit and gifts	63
II. ii. 173	You are a fishmonger	15
II. ii. 325	What players are they?	23
II. ii. 497	Livery Companies theme	18
	Julius Caesar	21
II. ii. 197	The satirical rogue	22
II. ii. 205	Though this be madness	22
II. ii. 362	Picture in little	24
II. ii. 365	If philosophy could find it out	24
II. ii. 377	Mad north-north-west	24
II. ii. 378	Hawk and handsaw	28
II. ii. 497	It shall to the barber's	19
II. ii. 520	The abstract and brief chronicles of the time	29
III. i. 143	I have heard of your paintings too	30
III. i. 145	Nicknaming of God's creatures	30
III. ii. 108	Polonius as Julius Caesar	31
III. ii. 138	Let the devil wear black…suit of sables	31
III. ii. 140	Build churches	33
III. ii. 144	Hobby-horse	33
III. iv. 25	Through the arras	36
IV. ii. 30	Hide fox, and all after	37
IV. v. 42	The owl was a baker's daughter	19 & 39
IV. v. 173	The false steward	40
IV. v. 184	Violets	40

IV. v. 187	Bonny sweet Robin	40
IV. vii. 80, 93	The Norman Lamord, Frenchman	42
V. i. 3	Make her grave straight	43
V. i. 12, 19, 48	Argal	45
V. i. 14	Goodman Delver	45
V. i. 15	Give me leave	45
V. i. 16	If the man . . . drown himself	46
V. i. 29	Come, my spade	19, 46
V. i. 29	There is no ancient gentlemen but Gardeners, ditchers and gravemakers	19, 44
V. i. 41	The mason, the shipwright, and carpenter	19
V. i. 60	Yaughan	46
V. i. 77	The pate of a politician	48
V. i. 83	Lord Such-a-one	48
V. i. 96	The skull of a lawyer	50
V. i. 135	Equivocation will undo us	50
V. i. 136	The age is grown so picked	52
V. i. 145	There the men are as mad as he	53
V. i. 165	A tanner will last you nine year	20
V. i. 181	Yorick	53
V. i. 293	A living monument	53
V. ii. 33	A baseness to write fair	54
V. ii. 74	And a man's life's no more than to say 'one'	57
V. ii. 80	Osrick	57
V. ii. 374	So shall you hear of carnal bloody and unnatural acts	58
V. ii. 378	All this can I truly deliver	59

ACKNOWLEDGEMENTS

In the first place I am much indebted to Ann Higgins who compiled earlier drafts, to John and Doreen Felix, who continued with my multiple afterthoughts and corrections, to my sons Michael and Antony, who filled in with suggestions for improvement, and most recently to Michael Legat for his particular skills and patience in preparing the whole venture for publication – a task that had at one time seemed to be beyond the time and effort at my disposal, and to his son Tony for preparing it for the printer.

Secondly I am grateful to Dr Peter Davison, Mrs Margaret Bartley, Dr L.G.Black, Christine, Lady Bett and other academics who, after reading through an earlier version, encouraged me to develop the theme I had taken up.

I have greatly benefited from the help and academic interest shown by Jim Sewell and staff at the London Guildhall Library and Archive; Robin Harcourt Williams, Archivist and Librarian at Hatfield House; Dr P.F.Palmer, Librarian, and Miss Barber, Archivist, at Lambeth Palace; and Bill Wood, Whitgift School Archivist.

F.H.G.P.